The Year's Scholarship: 1981

The Year's Scholarship in Science Fiction, Fantasy, and Horror Literature

1981

Edited by
MARSHALL B. TYMN

The Kent State University Press

Contents

Preface

The Year's Scholarship in Science Fiction, Fantasy, and Horror Literature is an ongoing, annotated secondary bibliography created to serve the needs of the scholarly community. The project first appeared as a series of annual installments in Extrapolation covering the period 1972-1979. These bibliographies, compiled by Roger C. Schlobin and me, were collected and published in book form by the Kent State University Press in 1979 and 1983.

So great has been the recent increase in scholarly attention to science fiction and fantasy that the bibliography has outgrown the confines of journal publication and is now being published as separate annual monographs. The new series has expanded its scope to include additional fan and semi-professional publications; criticism from the commercial science fiction magazines; and introductions to works of fiction, limited at this stage to the Gregg Press and Hyperion Press reprint titles, begun in the 1980 bibliography. This increased coverage was made possible by the conversion to the current editorial board, whose members collect and annotate the material for this bibliography. The initials of the annotator follow each entry.

The categories of The Year's Scholarship have been expanded from five to ten, providing easier access to its contents. The bibliography includes books, monographs, Ph.D. dissertations (with citations to Dissertation Abstracts International), scholarly reprints, periodical articles, essays in critical anthologies, and instructional media. Book reviews and letters are not included. Articles relevant to the bibliography are taken from the scholarly, library, and educational periodicals; general magazines; professional science fiction magazines; and the following major, established fan, semi-professional, and professional nonfiction publications in the fields of science fiction, fantasy, and horror literature: August Derleth Society Newsletter, Chesterton Review, Cinefantastique, CSL: The Bulletin of the New York C. S. Lewis Society, Dark Horizons (British), Extrapolation, Fantasy Commentator, Fantasy Macabre, Fantasy Newsletter, Foundation (British), Kalki: Studies in James Branch Cabell, Locus, Lovecraft Studies, Mervyn Peake Review, Mythlore, Nyctalops, Patchin Review, Philosophical Speculations, P*S*F*Q, Quartz (British), Riverside Quarterly, The Romantist, Science Fiction (Australia), Science Fiction Review, Science-Fiction Studies, SF Commentary (Australia), SFWA Bulletin, Starline, Starship, Thrust, and Vector (British).

Cross-references to significant author mentions in all sections of the bibliography are included in the Individual Author Studies sections after the name of the subject author. Co-authors of articles and books are also cross-referenced. All entries have access code numbers, which appear in the author and title indexes in place of page numbers.

The Year's Scholarship attempts to locate and annotate the relevant scholarship published each year in the United States. Coverage is thorough and comprehensive, and except for items in certain fan magazines not routinely surveyed by the editorial board, this bibliography is reasonably complete. We also include as much British, Canadian, and Australian scholarship as possible, although our coverage of these countries is more selective. No foreign-language scholarship is included, unless it has been published in English translations.

Any articles or books missed during a given year will be annotated and included in subsequent issues of the bibliography, as they are located. A particular problem has been the late publication of the MLA International Bibliography, one of our major library sources. Although many of the articles cited in MLA are listed in other, more current library indexes, some are not. As we locate these articles they will be annotated and included in later issues of The Year's Scholarship.

It is not our purpose to review, analyze, or judge the scholarship contained in this bibliography (although occasional subjective comments do sometimes appear); our annotations are designed to furnish the reader with content descriptions of each title. This information should serve the scholar in many ways: as an aid to individual research, as a guide to personal or library acquisition, and as a comprehensive survey of current trends in science fiction, fantasy, and horror scholarship.

Our plans for future issues include further refinements in the table of contents, better coverage of British fanzines, and the inclusion of more introductions to works of fiction. Your ideas and suggestions on how these three areas might be better implemented are most welcome.

We would also appreciate assistance from scholars and researchers furnishing us with materials for inclusion in The Year's Scholarship. Notices of articles, essays, and monographs, especially those appearing in sources not routinely covered in this bibliography, should be sent to the editor at 721 Cornell, Ypsilanti, MI 48197, U.S.A.

I would like to express my gratitude to the members of the editorial board, who have worked diligently and with a great deal of professional competence in compiling this bibliography. I would also like to thank Paul H. Rohmann, Director of the Kent State University Press, for his willingness to publish The Year's Scholarship in this new format.

Marshall B. Tymn

A. Bibliography and Reference

A01   Angenot, Mark, and Nadia Khouri. "An International
      Bibliography of Prehistoric Fiction." <u>SFS</u>, 8 (1981),
      38-53.
            A carefully selected list of fictions dealing
      with prehistoric man and/or lost worlds. The
      required characteristic is that some consistency
      with Darwinian theory and modern palaeontology be
      maintained. Appended is a list of related genre and
      narrative formulae. An introduction comments on the
      remarkable number of such fictions since about 1860.
      (DMH)

A02   Ashley, Mike, with Terry Jeeves. <u>The Complete Index
      to Astounding/Analog: Being An Index to the 50 years
      of Astounding Stories-Astounding SF & Analog: Janu-
      ary 1930 December 1979 Together with the Analog
      Annual, the Analog Yearbook, & the John W. Campbell
      Memorial Anthology.</u> Oak Forest, IL: Robert Weinberg,
      1981.
            An index to all fiction, nonfiction, art, and
      letters contained in this important magazine.
      Access is by issue, author, title, artist, and
      letter. Not only is this the most extensive mag-
      azine index ever compiled, it also enables research-
      ers to identify and locate material that has never
      before been systematically listed in any form. The
      standard reference to <u>Astounding/Analog</u>. (MBT)

A03   Barron, Neil, ed. <u>Anatomy of Wonder: A Critical
      Guide to Science Fiction</u>. 2nd ed. New York and
      London, 1981.
            This guide critically annotates almost 1,700
      English language books, adult and young adult, fic-
      tion and nonfiction. Essays precede the annotations
      and provide the historical and critical contexts.
      Additional coverage includes chapters on classroom
      aids, film and TV, science fiction illustration, and
      the magazines. A core collection checklist uses the
      expertise of contributors and outside readers.
      <u>Anatomy</u> is the major source for content descriptions
      of novels, anthologies, and single-author collec-
      tions in the science fiction field. Also issued in
      paperback. (MBT)

A04   -------. "Secrets from the Vault: Building a Per-
      sonal Reference Library." <u>FN</u>, No. 40 (1981), pp.
      23-27.

Discusses basic reference tools in science fiction and fantasy, with a selected bibliography of
essential works. (JS)

A05   Bates, Susannah. The Pendex: An Index of Pen Names
       and House Names in Fantastic, Thriller, and Series
       Literature. New York and London: Garland Publish-
       ing, 1981.
          Contains listings of real names, pen names, house
       names, collaborative pen names, and Stratemeyer
       Syndicate names. Two appendixes provide brief
       discussions of pulps and round robin serials.
       Should be used in conjunction with Barry McGhan's
       Sciencefiction and Fantasy Pseudonyms (Misfit Press,
       1976). (MBT)

A06   Berman, Ruth. "A Bibliography of Fantasy and Fan-
       tasy-Criticism in Four Leading Nineteenth-Century
       Periodicals." Extrapolation, 22 (1981), 277-90.
          Not annotated, but grouped by periodical:
       Blackwood's Edinburgh Magazine, Fraser's Magazine
       for Town and Country, The Cornhill Magazine, and
       The Edinburgh Review (criticism only). (JS)

A07   Boyajian, Jerry, and Kenneth R. Johnson. Index to
       The Science Fiction Magazines: 1979. Cambridge, MA:
       Twaci Press, 1981 pbk.
          The first in a series of retroactive indexes.
       All professionally published magazines devoted
       entirely or primarily to science fiction and fantasy
       are listed. Includes complete contents of each
       issue, including nonfiction. Access is by magazine
       title, author, and story title. Also included is an
       artist index. (MBT)

A08   -------. Index to the Science Fiction Magazines:
       1980. Cambridge, MA: Twaci Press, 1981 pbk.
          Begins the indexing of current science fiction
       magazines (see description of contents in preceding
       annotation). Includes an appendix of science
       fiction in miscellaneous magazines.

A09   Cowart, David, and Thomas L. Wymer, eds.
       Twentieth-Century American Science-Fiction Writers.
       Vol. 8 of Dictionary of Literary Biography. 2 vols.
       Detroit: Gale Research, 1981.
          Contains bio-critical studies of ninety authors
       who began writing after 1900 and before 1970. Each
       essay provides up-to-date biographical material
       together with a synthesis of the critical response
       to the author's major works and includes a chrono-
       logical list of most of the subject author's books,
       a selective bibliography of the author's short fic-
       tion, and secondary material about the author.
       Appendixes discuss such topics as the New Wave, sci-
       ence fantasy, science fiction art, paperback science
       fiction, science fiction films, fandom and conven-
       tions, fanzines, awards, magazines and anthologies,

and books for further reading (secondary). The
generally sound and well-balanced critical evalu-
ations make this work an excellent starting point
for new teachers. (MBT)

A10   DeVore, Howard (See A13)

A11   Fletcher, Marilyn P. Science Fiction Story Index:
       1950-1979. 2nd ed. Chicago: American Library
       Association, 1981 pbk.
            In view of the existence of William Contento's
       Index to Science Fiction Anthologies and Collections
       (G. K. Hall, 1978), this work should not have been
       published. Moreover, it is an incredibly inept
       compilation, indicating Fletcher's lack of knowledge
       of the science fiction field and poor skills as a
       compiler. (MBT)

A12   Fonstad, Karen Wynn. The Atlas of Middle-earth.
       Boston: Houghton Mifflin, 1981.
            Drawings on the text of The Silmarillion, The
       Hobbit, and The Lord of the Rings. Virtually every
       locatable place mentioned in these works appears on
       one or more of the 115 two-colored maps, and all the
       names are cross-referenced. The accompanying ex-
       planatory text is specific and thorough; the chrono-
       logical format of the book furnishes sequential
       informatin on Tolkien's works. The most detailed
       and meticulously researched and executed Tolkien
       atlas ever prepared. (MBT)

A13   Franson, Donald, and Howard DeVore. A History of
       the Hugo, Nebula, and International Fantasy Awards.
       Rev. ed. Dearborn, MI: Misfit Press, 1981 pbk.
            This enlarged and updated edition provides de-
       tailed information on the Hugo and Nebula Awards
       through 1981. Both the winners and the nominees in
       all categories are listed. Includes an author
       index.

A14   [Frazier, Robert]. "Speculative Poetry: Selected
       Resources." The Portland Review, 27 (Fall-Winter
       1981), 64.
            A vital core bibliography of an emerging field by
       its preeminent scholar, editor, and poet. (SE)

A15   Hall, Hal W. Science Fiction Book Review Index,
       1974-1979. Detroit: Gale Research, 1981.
            A complete record of all science fiction and
       fantasy books reviewed in nearly 250 general and
       specialized periodicals, providing access to 15,600
       reviews of 6,220 books. Review citations are ar-
       ranged alphabetically by author and are cross-
       referenced in a title index. Continued in annual
       supplements. (MBT)

A16   -------. SFBRI: Science Fiction Book Review Index.
       Vol. 11, 1980. Bryan, TX: SFBRI, 1981 pbk.

Annual index to science fiction and fantasy book reviews appearing in the commercial science fiction magazines, selected fanzines, and general and library-oriented magazines. Provides access to 2,316 reviews of 1,163 fiction and nonfiction books. (MBT)

A17   -------. Science Fiction Research Index. Vol. 1. Bryan, TX: SFBRI, 1981 pbk.
The first supplement to Hall's Science Fiction Index: Criticism (1980), an experimental indexing and accessing system to science fiction and fantasy scholarship, available on computer output microfiche. SFRI updates the file through 1980 and picks up older material that was not in the original file. Designed to provide subject access to all aspects of the science fiction and fantasy genres, the index is still under development. Entries are arranged into two sections: subject index and author index. Annotations are not provided. (MBT)

A18   Hopkins, Mariane S., ed. Fandom Directory. Langley AFB, VA: Fandom Computer Services, 1981 pbk.
A listing of over 8,000 names of fans, fan publications, clubs and organizations, specialty dealers, and conventions. Contains addresses and interest codes for fans and dealers, descriptive annotations for fanzines and clubs, geographical breakdowns for dealers, and a monthly calendar for conventions. Extra features include a fandom glossary and six articles on fan culture. The most comprehensive guide of its type. (MBT)

A19   Jeeves, Terry (See A02)

A20   Johnson, Kenneth R. (See A07, A08)

A21   Justice, Keith L. "A Failed Experiment--The Laser Books: History and Checklist." SFC, No. 15 (1981), pp. 4-7.
Analysis and bibliography of a short-lived science fiction line. (MBT)

A22   Kemp, G. R. "An Index to Vortex." Quartz, 1 (December 1981), 13-15.
Vortex was a short-lived British magazine which appeared in 1977 and ran for only five issues. Contents are listed by issue and by author. There is also a listing of cover artwork by issue, citing name of artist and title of work. Interior artwork is listed by artist, citing story title and page number. (JF)

A23   Khouri, Nadia (See A01)

A24   Reginald, R. Science Fiction & Fantasy Awards. San Bernardino, CA: Borgo Press, 1981 pbk.

Complete checklists of the following awards:
Hugo, Nebula, Locus, Jupiter, Pilgrim International
Fantasy, Ditmar, August Derleth, World Fantasy,
Eaton, Gandalf, British Fantasy, John W. Cambell
Memorial, Milford, Prometheus, and selected foreign
awards. Includes an index to winners.

A25   Schlobin, Roger C. "The Fulfillment of the Dawn: A
Checklist of Women Science-Fiction Writers,
1950-1980." New Moon, 1 (Winter 1981-82), 4-17.
   Lists five hundred titles within the period,
noting that 1950 is the date of publication of Fury,
by C. L. Moore and Henry Kutner, a work which ushers
in a flood of science fiction by women writers.
Includes adult and juvenile science fiction titles.
Not annotated, but listed "in reading order." Citations of anthologies is limited to those that
focus completely on women writers. (TPD)

A26   -------. "The Future Females: A Selected Checklist
through 1979." In Future Females: A Critical An-
thology. Ed. Marlene S. Barr. Bowling Green, OH:
Bowling Green State Univ. Popular Press, 1981, pp.
179-89.
   Lists some five hundred science fiction works by
women writers published mostly in the 1960s and
1970s but includes earlier works like Gilman's
Herland (1915) and Shelley's Frankenstein (1818).
Only first editions are listed in most cases. (TPD)

A27   -------, and Marshall B. Tymn. "The Year's Scholarship in Science Fiction and Fantasy: 1979." Extrapolation, 22 (1981), 25-91.
   Last magazine appearance of this annual bibliography covering all American and selected British
criticism. (JS)

A28   Smith, Curtis C., ed. Twentieth-Century Science-
Fiction Writers. New York: St. Martin's, 1981. A
reference handbook which furnishes information for
about six hundred English-language science fiction
writers, selected for inclusion by a distinguished
advisory board of scholars. Each entry includes a
brief biographical sketch, a comprehensive bibliography, and a signed critical profile. Two appendixes cover thirty-five foreign-language science
fiction writers whose works have been translated
into English, and five major fantasy writers.
Valuable for the scope of its coverage and its
currency. Effectively supersedes the the bio-
bibliographical profiles in Brian Ash, Who's Who in
Science Fiction (Taplinger, 1976), Baird Searles, A
Reader's Guide to Science Fiction (Avon, 1979) and
much of Donald Tuck, The Encyclopedia of Science
Fiction and Fantasy Through 1968 (Advent, 1974,
1978). (MBT)

A29   Swain, Gunter E.   "A Supplement to: <u>Thirty Years of</u>
        <u>Arkham House</u>."   <u>August Derleth Soc News</u>, 5 (1981),
        9-10.
            An update of Derleth's 1970 book, <u>Thirty Years of</u>
        <u>Arkham House 1939-1969</u>; Swain's article is a check-
        list of authors and titles from 1970-1981. (SE)

A30   Tymn, Marshall B.   (See also A27)

A31   -------.   "Fantasy Literature: A Survey."
        <u>Analytical & Enumerative Bibliography</u>, 5 (1981),
        25-34.
            Surveys the important works of fantasy reference,
        from the first time such works began to be published
        to the current state of the art, for those who wish
        to pursue research in the field. Divided into the
        following sections: general bibliographies, author
        bibliographies, magazine indexes, anthology indexes,
        film bibliographies, and bibliographies of secondary
        works. (MBT)

A32   -------, ed.   <u>Horror Literature: A Core Collection</u>
        <u>and Reference Guide</u>. New York and London: R. R.
        Bowker, 1981.
            The first reference book ever compiled for horror
        fiction, poetry, and the pulp magazines. Contains
        over 1,300 annotated primary and secondary titles.
        The historical essays that introduce each chapter
        outline the growth of horror literature in England
        and America from its origins in the Gothic romance
        to its manifestations in contemporary literature. A
        reference section provides complete coverage of
        related scholarship, periodicals, organizations,
        awards, and research collections. Also issued in
        paperback. (MBT)

A33   -------, ed.   <u>The Science Fiction Reference Book: A</u>
        <u>Comprehensive Handbook and Guide to the History,</u>
        <u>Literature, Scholarship, and Related Activities of</u>
        <u>the Science Fiction and Fantasy Fields</u>. Mercer
        Island, WA: Starmont House, 1981 pbk.
            Contains a variety of background information on
        the field as a whole, combined with practical infor-
        mation such as reading lists and resource materials.
        Intended as an introduction to fantastic literature
        and its activities for the teacher and fan. Cover-
        age is broad and comprehensive. (MBT)

A34   Wymer, Thomas L., ed.   (See A09)

B. General Surveys and Histories

B01　Aiken, Arnold. "You Can Get There from Here."
Vector, No. 101 (1981), pp. 14-17.
　　　Considers the relationship between science fiction and other popular literary genres such as crime
fiction, which also had a pulp tradition. (JF)

B02　Asimov, Isaac. Asimov on Science Fiction. Garden
City, NY: Doubleday, 1981.
　　　A collection of fifty-five brief essays on a wide
range of science fiction topics arranged in eight
sections: general, writing, predictions, history,
writers, fans, reviews, and Asimov. Consists of
material published during the 1970s and 1980s.
(MBT)

B03　-------. "Editorial: Science Fiction Anthologies."
IASFM (May 1981), pp. 6-10.
　　　A history of early science fiction anthologies
and of Asimov's own involvement in anthologies as
author and editor/compiler. (TWH)

B04　-------. "Editorial: Science Fiction Poetry." IASFM
(March 1981), pp. 6-11.
　　　Asimov's views on poetry, the sources of poetic
form, and their roles in modern literature, particularly science fiction. (TWH)

B05　Bayley, Barrington J. "The SF Novel and Basic Form"
Vector, No. 103 (1981), pp. 19-23.
　　　Discusses the use of formula in science fiction
and regards Philip K. Dick's Solar Lottery as the
structurally perfect novel. Diagrams are used to
illustrate the relationship between the characters
in the novel and in John Varley's Ophiuchi Hotline,
Charles Harness' The Paradox Man, and his own novel,
The Grand Wheel. (JF)

B06　Berman, Ruth. "Critical Reactions to Fantasy in Four
Nineteenth-Century Periodicals: Edinburgh Review,
Blackwood's, Fraser's and Cornhill." The Sphinx, 4,
No. 13 (1981), 1-37.
　　　Charts the reactions of critics throughout the
nineteenth century from tentative acceptance in the
1830s, outright condemnation in the 1870s, and
acceptance again at the close of the century. (TPD)

B07   Bova, Ben. "Building a Real World." <u>Rigel Science
       Fiction</u> (Fall 1981), pp. 16-19.
            An essay on the relationship between science
       fiction and mainstream literature, film, and the
       politics of space exploration. (TWH)

B08   Columbo, John Robert. "Four Hundred Years of Fan-
       tastic Literature in Canada." <u>Stardust</u> (Spring
       1981), pp. 39-48.
            A wide-ranging lecture on the contributions of a
       number of writers who used Canadian and Northern
       elements in their science fiction. (TPD)

B09   -------. "Science Fiction in Bulgaria." <u>SFS</u>, 8
       (1981), 187-90.
            A description of a flourishing science fiction in
       the Bulgarian language pieced together from an
       interview with the country's two leading science
       fiction writers, Pavel Vezinov and Ljuben Dilov.
       (DMH)

B10   Dautzenberg, J.A. "A Survey of Dutch and Flemish
       Science Fiction." <u>SFS</u>, 8 (1981), 173-86.
            After clearly setting out why Flemish literature
       forms a whole with Dutch, this article surveys
       fandom, the market for translated science fiction,
       and original science fiction in Dutch and Flemish.
       Contains a list of original Dutch and Flemish works
       about science fiction. (DMH)

B11   Dozois, Gardner. "Beyond the Golden Age." <u>Star-
       ship</u>, No. 42 (1981), pp. 7-13.
            In this general survey of the recent decades of
       science fiction, Dozois develops the notion that
       when anyone begins reading science fiction that
       starting point will become the Golden Age for that
       reader. Dozois then extrapolates from each gener-
       ation over the recent decades. (DMH)

B12   "Ghost Riders from Germany: An Early Phase of Fan-
       tasy Poetry." <u>The Portland Review</u> (Fall-Winter
       1981), pp. 47-48.
            Historical discussion of the eighteenth century
       "graveyard verse" and horror-ballad background,
       setting the stage for the English horror-ballad
       movement of the 1790s. Includes primary and second-
       ary bibliographies. (SE)

B13   Frazier, Robert, and Terry Hansen. "A Silent Evolu-
       tion: Speculative Verse." <u>P*S*F*Q</u>, No. 5 (1981), pp.
       10-13.
            Analyses the evolution of speculative verse, a
       subgenre that boasts a solid body of work. Features
       a selected bibliography of important poems. (JME)

B14   Hansen, Terry (See B13)

B15   Jonas, Gerald. "Science Fiction's Cosmic Horizon."
       <u>Science Digest</u>, 98 (October 1981), 120, 122.

A discussion of contemporary science fiction in which the laws of physics impose restrictions as well as give new freedom to imaginative writers. In many ways today's better science fiction becomes a teaching device for a public that has no other means to the scientific ideas shaping our future. (PA)

B16   Kaveny, Roz. "Science Fiction in the 1970s." Foundation, No. 22 (1981), pp. 5-35.
A freewheeling survey that discusses nearly all that is important in the English-language science fiction of the entire decade. (DMH)

B17   King Stephen. Danse Macabre. New York: Everest House, 1981.
A modern master evaluates horror in literature and the mass media, focusing on works produced in the United States and England from the 1950s to the present. Filled with insights into King's own writing and the influences which shaped his career. Two appendixes list one hundred films and one hundred books important to the genre. (MBT)

B18   Kuczka, Peter. "Science Fiction in Hungary." Foundation, No. 23 (1981), pp. 40-44.
A defense of the extent and vitality of modern science fiction in Hungarian, focusing on writers such as Frigyes Karinthy. (DMH)

B19   McCutcheon, Kathy. "Science and Fantasy in Science Fiction." Vector, No. 104 (1981), pp. 7-13.
Considers the question of how scientific the science is in science fiction. The subtle relationship between science and science fiction is discussed and the examples of hyperspace and artificial intelligence are used to support the view that few speculative ideas are in fact scientifically plausible because they depend on present knowledge. Most writers combine elements of fantasy, thus producing a science fiction that may be defined as a "fantasy that uses science as a source of ideas." (JF)

B20   Moskowitz, Sam. "Voyagers through Eternity: A History of Science Fiction From the Beginnings to H. G. Wells." Fantasy Commentator, 4 (1981), 127-45, 190-92.
Beginning with Greek utopian and fantastic adventure literature, this critical survey covers Lucian, Johannes Kepler, Francis Godwin, Cyrano de Bergerac, and Daniel Defoe. Science fiction authors and figures who were important influences on the genre are also covered. (JAG)

B21   Moylan, Thomas Patrick. "Figures of Hope: The Critical Utopia of the 1970's. The Revival, Destruction, and Transformation of Utopian Writing in

the United States: A Study of the Ideology, Structure, and Historical Context of Representative
Texts." Ph.D. dissertation, University of Wisconsin-
Milwaukee, 1981; DAI, 42: 2670A.
   Focusing on the novels, The Female Man by Joanna
Russ, The Dispossessed by Ursula K. Le Guin, Woman
on the Edge of Time by Marge Piercy, and Triton by
Samuel Delaney, this dissertation discusses the
modern phenomena of critical utopian writing which
deals less with the idealized utopia and more with
the process of building a utopian society. (PA)

B22   Nicholas, Joseph. "The Shape of Things to Come."
      Vector, No. 101 (1981), pp. 6-14.
         Argues that too much current science fiction is
      merely repeating overused formulas to satisfy public
      demand, and that this results in a lack of quality.
      Four emerging trends are discussed: the retreat into
      the ghetto, repetition of familiar themes, best-
      sellerism, and the struggle to reintegrate with the
      mainstream. (JF)

B23   Rowe, Nigel. A History of Science Fiction Fandom in
      New Zealand. Rothesay Bay, Auckland, New Zealand:
      Privately Printed, 1981 pbk.
         Not seen. (MBT)

B24   Van Helsing, Kurt [pseud. of T. E. D. Klein]. "Dr.
      Van Helsing's Handy Guide to Ghost Stories." The
      Twilight Zone (August 1981), pp. 69-75.
         Discusses primitive fears that give rise to a
      belief in ghosts and provides a short survey of the
      genre. (SE)

B25   -------. "Dr. Van Helsing's Handy Guide to Ghost
      Stories: Part II." The Twilight Zone (September
      1981), pp. 74-77.
         Considers whether or not a belief in the super-
      natural is crucial to writing or appreciating ghost
      fiction. (SE)

B26   -------. "Dr. Van Helsing's Handy Guide to Ghost
      Stories: Part III." The Twilight Zone (October
      1981), pp. 56-60.
         Addresses the aesthetics of the ghost story.
      Debates whether or not the genre is easy or dif-
      ficult to write. Argues that the tale is ideally
      short, but not too short because of the need to
      create atmosphere. (SE)

B27   -------. "Dr. Van Helsing's Handy Guide to Ghost
      Stories: Part IV." The Twilight Zone (November
      1981), pp. 62-66.
         Concluding installment of the light but erudite
      and insightful survey. Discusses the "pleasures" of
      the ghost story and the positive and negative as-
      pects of literary fear. Suggests that readers do
      not have to be wholly terrified by a tale to enjoy
      it. Points out the timelessness of the genre. (SE)

B28   Wilson, Andrew J.   "If It's Wednesday This Must Be
      Narnia: Exploring the Links between Phantasy and
      Reality." Dark Horizons, No. 24 (1981), pp. 19-23.
        A general survey of the many diverse fantasy
      worlds created by writers such as E. R. Eddison,
      Andre Norton, A. Merritt, and others. Themes dis-
      cussed include lost races, parallel worlds, and
      rites of passage. (JF)

C. Theoretical and Critical Studies

C01   Aldiss, Brian W. <u>This World and Nearer Ones: Essays Exploring the Familiar</u>. Kent, OH: Kent State Univ. Press, 1981 pbk.
    A collection of articles, reviews, and travel pieces linked by the author's penetrating wit and by the use of the theme of the complex unity of art and science which forms the inner mystery of science fiction. Reprint of the 1979 British edition. (MBT)

C02   ------, and Tom Shippey. <u>Science Fiction: Its Nature and Origins</u> (Track A) and <u>The Problems and Potentials of Science Fiction</u> (Track B) [cassette]. Mt. Vernon, NY: Audio Learning, 1979. Order #ELA058, $25.00.
    Aldiss and Shippey discuss origins, definitions, and potentials of science fiction and its differences from mainstream fiction. (AT)

C03   Barth, Melissa Ellen. "Problems in Generic Classification: Toward a Definition of Fantasy Fiction." Ph.D. dissertation, Purdue University, 1981; <u>DAI</u>, 42: 2125A.
    Proposes a method of identifying works belonging to the genre of fantasy fiction, termed "fabulation" by this author. An analysis is made of three significant generic markers: causation, narrative structure, and patterns of closure. (PA)

C04   Berger, Albert I. "Love, Death, and the Atomic Bomb: Sexuality and Community in Science Fiction." <u>SFS</u>, 8 (1981), 280-96.
    Argues that three inadequacies in early science fiction, its treatment of sexuality, characterization, and socio-political issues, are closely related and attributable in part to the strong commitment to scientific quest that was a major item of faith among science fiction writers. This early fundamentalism is balanced against an exploration of the personal and the intimate in the works of Sturgeon, Merril, and Moore toward the end of the period. (DMH)

C05   Blackford, Russell. "Myth and the Art of Science Fiction Commentary." <u>Science Fiction</u>, 3 (1981), 52-56.

Suggests some problems in the critical position
that science fiction is a return to the use of
archetypal mythic figures. (DMH)

C06   Brantlinger, Patrick. "The Gothic Origins of
Science Fiction." Novel, 12 (Fall 1980), 30-43.
Suggests that the central message of Gothic
romance, involving the power of assertion of the
irrational over the rational, is also the message of
science fiction. Both genres conjure up visions of
apocalyptic nightmare fantasy. (TPD)

C07   Brooke-Rose, Christine. A Rhetoric of the Unreal:
Studies in Narrative and Structure, Especially of
the Fantastic. New York and London: Cambridge Univ.
Press, 1981.
A study of the wide range of fiction, from short
stories to tales of horror, from fairy tales and
romances to science fiction, to which the rather
loose term "fantastic" has often been applied.
Cutting across this wide field, the author examines
the essential differences between these types of
narrative against the background of realistic fiction. Bibliography. (MBT)

C08   Delany, Samuel R. "The Discourse of Science Fiction." SFWA Bulletin, No. 76 (1981), pp. 27-35.
Beginning with a description of a fan convention
at which there was a critic Guest of Honor, Delany
argues that criticism must analyze and understand
the basic "workings" of criticism, or discourse,
itself. (DMH)

C09   -------. "Some Reflections on SF Criticism." SFS,
8 (1981), 233-39.
An expression of regret at the counterproductive
use in science fiction criticism of a rhetoric from
traditional literary genres and an updating of his
1968 paper, "About 5,750 Words," on the peculiar
rhetoric found in science fiction. (DMH)

C10   Garey, Terry A. "The Persnicketiness of Communication." Aurora (Summer 1981), pp. 11-13.
A discussion of how an aesthetic towards
femininism might be established in science fiction
poetry. (TWH)

C11   Jackson, Rosemary. Fantasy: The Literature of
Subversion. New York and London: Methuen, 1981.
An argument against vague interpretation of
fantasy as mere escapism. Seeks to define fantasy
as a distinct kind of narrative. Following a
general theoretical section which introduces recent
work on fantasy, Jackson explores literary fantasies
from the Gothic tale of terror to twentieth-century
dystopias, locating fantasy in between the related
forms of fairy tales and science fiction. Sees
fantasy as primarily an expression of unconscious

drives and as a historically determined form whose
ambiguities are seen as expressing cultural unease.
Also issued in paperback. (MBT)

C12   Landow, George P. "And the World Became Strange:
Realms of Literary Fantasy." Georgia Review, 33
(1979), 7-42.
      Sets forth a general literary definition of
fantasy and examines characteristics of literary
fantasy since 1850 in representative works by
Ruskin, MacDonald, Meredith, Morris, and Hodgson.
Also proposes fantasy as another literary tradition,
"a capable and compelling alternative to the realistic novel," running from the German Marchen
through Carlyle, MacDonald, Carroll, and Morris to
Lewis, Lindsay, and Tolkien. (JAG)

C13   Larson, David M. "Thematic Structure and Conventions in Science Fiction." The Sphinx, No. 13
(1981), pp. 38-47.
      Argues for the importance of convention in
several works of social science fiction, including
three dystopian novels by John Brunner, Katherine
MacLean's Missing Man, and Ursula K. Le Guin's The
Dispossessed. (TPD)

C14   Law, Richard. "Science Fiction: The Urgency of
Style." Extrapolation, 22 (1981), 325-33.
      Comments on the effect of style in Le Guin's The
Left Hand of Darkness, Godwin's "The Cold Equa-
tions," and Russ's "When It Changed." (JS)

C15   Lem, Stanislaw. "Metafantasia: The Possibilities of
Science Fiction." Trans. Etelka de Laczay and
Istvan Csicsery-Ronay. SFS, 8 (1981), 54-71.
      The first English translation of the concluding
chapter of Lem's Fantastyka y Futurologia (SF and
Futurology, 1970), a theoretical work that has had
an important influence on Darko Suvin, Robert
Scholes, and other scholars. (DMH)

C16   Messent, Peter B., ed. Literature of the Occult: A
Collection of Critical Essays. Englewood Cliffs,
NJ: Prentice-Hall, 1981.
      By examining the Anglo-American literary tradi-
tion from the eighteenth century to the present,
this collection enumerates the reasons for the
appearance of the occult in fiction and the particular thematic interests associated with the genre.
Selected bibliography. Also issued in paperback.
[Contents not annotated.] (MBT)

C17   Mitchison, Naomi. "The Profession of Science
Fiction, 23: Wonderful Deathless Ditties."
Foundation, No. 21 (1981), pp. 27-34.
      Theorizes about the moral and prophetic strain in
science fiction cast as personal reflections about
her many conversations with Stapledon, in particular, and also with her brother. (DMH)

C18   Montgomery, Marion. "The Prophetic Poet and the
       Loss of Middle Earth." Georgia Review, 33 (1979),
       66-83.
           Contends that writers until Tolkien, under the
       influence of rationalism, substituted the absurd and
       grotesque for the imaginative and the transcendent.
       Discusses works by Chesterton, Orwell, Hawthorne,
       Swift, Tolkien, and Flannery O'Connor. (JAG)

C19   Morse, Donald E. "Masterpieces of Garbage: Martin
       Tropp and Science Fiction." CEA Critic, 43 (1980),
       14-17.
           Responds to Tropp's article (see C32), taking
       Tropp to task for a severely limited definition of
       "good" literature. (JAG)

C20   Moss, Anita. "Crime and Punishment--or Develop-
       ment--in Fairy Tales and Fantasy." Mythlore, No. 27
       (1981), pp. 26-28, 42.
           Discusses didactic purpose of some fantasies for
       young people that actually are designed to terrify
       readers into clinging to adult values. Ronald
       Dahl's Charlie and the Chocolate Factory is a modern
       example, as Andrew Lang's The Gold of Fairnilee and
       Natalie Babbitt's Tuck Everlasting are examples of
       fantasy stories that let children grow without
       intimidation. (JS)

C21   Nagl, Manfred. "National Peculiarities in German
       Science Fiction: Science Fiction as a National and
       Topical Literature." Trans. Robert Philmus. SFS, 8
       (1981), 29-34.
           Theorizes that assumptions about the ahistorical
       and cross-national nature of science fiction are
       propagated by the U.S. mass media and are innac-
       curate; suggests characteristics be determined by
       nation and location. Focuses on German particular-
       ities from 1980 to 1965. (DMH)

C22   Panshin, Alexei, and Cory Panshin. "Science Fiction
       and the Dimension of Myth." Extrapolation, 22
       (1981), 127-39.
           Using the monomyth of heroic quest as described
       by Joseph Campbell in The Hero with a Thousand
       Faces, this article discusses the "region of
       supernatural wonder" where the hero must be tested,
       as pictured in science fiction stories compared to
       myths and Sufi texts. (JS)

C23   Panshin, Cory (See C22)

C24   Paulson, Ronald. "Gothic Fiction and the French
       Revolution." ELH, 48 (1982), 532-54.
           Describes how ideas and fears generated by the
       French Revolution--i.e. liberation, reform, tyranny,
       the reign of terror--are reflected in certain Gothic
       novels of that period. Particular attention is

given to <u>The Monk</u> by M. G. Lewis; <u>Things as They</u>
<u>Are; or the Adventures of Caleb Williams</u> by William
Godwin; and <u>Frankenstein</u> by Mary Shelley. (PA)

C25   Rose, Mark. <u>Alien Encounters: Anatomy of Science</u>
       <u>Fiction</u>. Cambridge, MA: Harvard Univ. Press, 1981.
         An assessment of science fiction as a genre.
       Rose suggests that the human is the human in rela-
       tion to the nonhuman. The nonhuman may be projected
       into space, as an alien being or a form of inanimate
       nature, or into some future or alternate time; it
       may be a literal or metaphorical machine; or it may
       be found within the human. Rose's continuing themes
       include science fiction as a form of romance, as a
       mediator between the conviction of free will and the
       conviction of determinism, as a displacement of
       essentially religious concerns, as as a mirror of
       various aspects of the alienated sensibility of the
       modern era. Also issued in paperback. (MBT)

C26   Schlobin, Roger C. "The Fool and the Fantastic."
       <u>FN</u>, No. 43 (1981), pp. 6-9, 29.
         At first, it seems unlikely that the rather dour
       field of heroic fantasy, concerned with right vs.
       wrong and with setting up clear boundaries between
       the two, could accomodate the character of the wise
       fool who calls rigid absolutes into question by his
       antics. Schlobin, however, finds the fool in many
       examples of modern fantasy, in particular, works by
       Harlan Ellison, Italo Calvino, L. Sprague de Camp,
       Charles G. Finney, Roger Zelazny, and Peter S.
       Beagle. (JS)

C27   Schwartz, Richard Alan. "Thomas Pynchon and the
       Evolution of Fiction." <u>SFS</u>, 8 (1981), 165-72.
         A discussion of experimental authors, focusing on
       Pynchon, suggesting how mainstream literature might
       come to coincide with science fiction through a
       disavowal of realism by the use of contemporary
       scientific principles and playfulness. (DMH)

C28   Shippey, Tom (See C02)

C29   Smith, John. "Post STS-1 Fiction." <u>PR</u>, No. 1
       (1981), pp. 16-17.
         Criticizes science fiction for holding on to
       outdated scientific concepts, and failing to explore
       ideas that <u>are</u> freshly promising. (JS)

C30   Tem, Steve Rasnic. "On Defining & Not Defining
       Speculative Poetry." <u>Starline</u>, No. 5 (1981), pp.
       12-15.
         A theoretical consideration of the relationship
       between science, myth, speculation, and poetry,
       taking the meaning of each of these as given and
       understood, although the area where they intersect,
       which forms the basis for speculative poetry, may
       not be. (TWH)

C31   Thompson, Hilary. "Doorways to Fantasy." Canadian
       Children's Literature, 21 (1981), 8-16.
            Examines the narrative devices ("doorways") by
       means of which fantasy characters move from our
       world into the world of fantasy, its echo. Con-
       siders Alan Garner, Madeleine L'Engle, William
       Mayne, C. S. Lewis, Susan Cooper, and two Canadian
       writers, Ruth Nichols and Catherine Anthony. (TPD)

C32   Tropp, Martin. "It Came from Inner Space: Science
       Fiction and the Self." CEA Critic, 42 (1980),
       20-24.
            In his literature course, Tropp sees science
       fiction as a vehicle to entice students into appre-
       ciating literature. Its appeal lies in the fact
       that good science fiction is close to medieval
       literature in theme and content (adventure, quests,
       strange landscapes, threatening aliens, etc.).
       (JAG)

C33   Wilt, Judith. "The Imperial Mouth: Imperialism, the
       Gothic and Science Fiction." Journal of Popular
       Culture, 14 (1981), 618-28.
            Through a discussion of works of the Victorian
       era such as Dracula by Bram Stoker and H.G. Wells's
       The War of the Worlds, this essay theorizes that the
       imperialism of the era was a contributing force in
       the mutation of Gothic literature into science
       fiction. (PA)

C34   Wingrove, David. "Saving the Tale." Vector, No.
       101 (1981), pp. 21-29.
            Examines the problem involved in attempting to
       distinguish science fiction from mainstream litera-
       ture and the inadequacy of definitions such as Brian
       Aldiss' in his Billion Year Spree. Criticism from
       both within and outside the genre is used to
       identify the distinguishing elements of science
       fiction and to consider the relevance of criticism.
       The views of Samuel Delany and Ursula Le Guin are
       compared, and the role of the critic is also dis-
       cussed. (JF)

C35   Wolfe, Gene. "What Do They Mean, SF?" SFWA
       Bulletin, No. 75 (1981), pp. 20-25.
            Charming distinctions, with examples, among the
       terms "science fiction," "speculative fiction," and
       "science fantasy." Originally published in The
       Writer (1980). (DMH)

C36   Yolen, Jane. Touch Magic: Fantasy, Faerie and
       Folklore in the Literature of Childhood. New York:
       Philomel, 1981.
            A collection of essays on the importance of
       fairytale and fantasy. Beginning with a brief
       history of folk literature and fairytales, Yolen
       then discusses their functions in the social, emo

tional, and intellectual growth of children. She
then points out the vital roles played by fantasy in
the stimulation of the imagination and the acquisition of language. (MBT)

D. Subject Studies

D01   Barr, Marleen S., ed. <u>Future Females: A Critical
       Anthology</u>. Bowling Green, OH: Bowling Green State
       Univ. Popular Press, 1981.
            Anthology of fifteen essays about the changing
       roles of women as writers of and characters in
       science fiction and utopian visions. Contents:
       "Science Fiction Women Before Liberation" by Eric S.
       Rabkin; "Alexei Panshin's Almost Non-Sexist <u>Rite of
       Passage</u>" by Anne Hudson Jones; "She Pluck'd, She
       Eat" by James D. Merritt; "Woman as Nature in Sci-
       ence Fiction" by Scott Sanders; "Coming Home: Four
       Feminist Utopias and Patriarchal Experience" by
       Carol Pearson; "Recent Feminist Utopias" by Joanna
       Russ; "A Footnote to Russ's 'Recent Feminist Uto-
       pias'" by Robert Scholes; "An Ambiguous Legacy: The
       Role and Position of Women in the English Eutopia"
       by Lyman Tower Sargent; "A Woman Appeared" by Suzy
       McKee Charnas; "In and Out of Time: The Form of
       Marge Piercy's Novels" by Susan Kress; "You, U.K. Le
       Guin" by Norman N. Holland; "Charles Bronson,
       Samurai, and Other Feminine Images: A Transactive
       Response to <u>The Left Hand of Darkness</u>" by Marleen S.
       Barr; "A Female Captain's Enterprise: The Implica-
       tions of <u>Star Trek</u>'s 'Turnabout Intruder'" by Edward
       Whetmore; "A Personal Response to Whetmore's 'A
       Female Captain's Enterprise'" by Arthur Asa Berger;
       "Where's All the Fiction in Science Fiction?" and
       "The Future Females" [bibliography] by Roger C.
       Schlobin. [The contents of <u>Future Females</u> are
       individually annotated elsewhere in this bibliog-
       raphy.] (MBT)

D02   Berman, Jeffrey. "Where's All the Fiction in
       Science Fiction?" In <u>Future Females</u>. Ed. Marleen
       S. Barr. Bowling Green, OH: Bowling Green State
       Univ. Popular Press, 1981, pp. 164-76.
            After pointing out that science fiction seldom
       treats the nature of fiction or art in future time,
       Berman examines several works--mainly by women
       writers--which make some attempt to do so. (TPD)

D03   Braswell, Laurel. "The Visionary Voyage in Science
       Fiction and Medieval Allegory." <u>Mosaic</u>, 14 (Winter
       1981), 125-42.
            Explores the motif of the visionary voyage in
       modern works by Zelazny, Delany, and Le Guin, and in

medieval allegories by Chaucer, Dante, Prudentius,
and others, showing that all narratives considered
present "continuing conceits" of spiritual truth in
fictional form. (TPD)

D04   Byrd, Donald. "Science Fiction's Intelligent Com-
        puters." Byte, 6 (September 1981), 200ff.
             Takes a close look at science fiction novels
        which feature intelligent computers. The author
        feels that many science fiction writers, though not
        all, lack understanding of how computers work as
        well as the nature of intelligence--machine or
        otherwise. Two science fiction novels are given
        particular attention: The Adolescence of P-1 by
        Thomas Ryan and The Two Faces of Tomorrow by James
        Hogan. (PA)

D05   Chamberlain, Gordon B. (See D15)

D06   Corley, James. "Serpent in the Garden." Arena, No.
        12 (1981), pp. 4-9.
             Uses Blish as a spokesman for science fiction's
        rediscovery of religion as a possible subject for
        fiction. (JS)

D07   Dean, John. "The Science Fiction City." Founda-
        tion, No. 23 (1981), pp. 64-72.
             A schematic discussion of the way the city as
        image helps the mind of the future take form in
        science fiction, touching on important texts from
        Wells's The Sleeper Awakes to recent 1980 fictions.
        (DMH)

D08   Dunn, Thomas P., and Richard D. Erlich. "A Vision
        of Dystopia: Beehives and Mechanization." Journal
        of General Education, 32 (Spring 1981), 45-57.
             Discusses several nightmare visions to show that
        the Elizabethan utopian concept of the hive-state
        has become a modern dystopian archetype. (TPD)

D09   Erlich, Richard D. (See D08)

D10   Flanery, Karen, and Nana Grasmick. Fandom Is for
        the Young: Or One Convention Too Many. New York:
        Vantage Press, 1981.
             Anecdotes on fans and fandom written by two
        housewives who became active fans. (MBT)

D11   Frasier, Brian M. "The Future: Subject to Change
        without Notice." Amazing (May 1981), pp. 125-30.
             A study of satire in science fiction, concen-
        trating on Frederick Pohl and Lester Del Rey's
        collaborative novel, Preferred Risk. (TWH)

D12   Frost, Brian J. "Her Ways Are Death: A Study of
        Feminine Evil in Myth and Literature." Dark
        Horizons, No. 24 (1981), pp. 21-23, 27.

Beginning with a brief examination of various
demonic female beings from ancient literature and
mythology, this study then examinies their appearance in both nineteenth- and twentieth-century
novels such as M. P. Shiel's Hugenin's Wife and Jack
Mann's The Ninth Life. Novels of witchcraft are
also discussed. (JF)

D13   Fulmer, Gilbert. "Time Travel, Determinism, and
       Fatalism." PS, 1 (March 1981), 41-48.
       Considers philosophical complications of time
travel (referring to Asimov's The End of Eternity
and Bayley's The Fall of Chronopolis), in particular
the question of whether knowledge of a future situ-
ation makes it impossible to act to prevent that
future happening. (JS)

D14   Grasmick, Nana (See D10)

D15   Hacker, Barton C., and Gordon B. Chamberlain.
       "Pasts That Might Have Been: An Annotated Bibliog-
       raphy of Alternate History." Extrapolation, 22
       (1981), 334-78.
       A list of works showing alterations in history as
we know it; arranged alphabetically by author. (JS)

D16   Harvey, John M. "A Vampire by Any Other Name."
       Dark Horizons, No. 22 (1981), pp. 15-19.
       Considers the possibility that vampire legends
existed in Britain as well as on the continent.
(JF)

D17   Hurwood, Bernhardt J. Vampires. New York and
       London: Quick Fox, 1981 pbk.
       Fully illustrated with drawings, paintings, and
movie stills, this popular treatment explains the
"cultural differences" among vampires who have
appeared throughout history in various parts of the
world. The author profiles the personalities of the
past and present vampires and explores the future of
the vampire and changing social attitudes toward
what is now considered the world's favorite monster.
Included is a list of vampire-related organizations,
a secondary bibliography, and a filmography. (MBT)

D18   Jones, Anne Hudson. "Alexei Panshin's Almost Non-
       Sexist Rite of Passage." In Future Females. Ed.
       Marleen S. Barr. Bowling Green, OH: Bowling Green
       State Univ. Popular Press, 1981, pp. 26-33.
       Panshin's science fiction novel offers an alter-
native to the traditional American literary pattern
which consigns female characters to "woman's work"
after initiation into adult life. (TPD)

D19   Leiber, Justin. "On Science Fiction and Philos-
       ophy." PS, 1 (March 1981), 5-11.
       Philosophers and science fiction writers both
build constructions having (perhaps) some relevance

to reality--but the activity of creating coherent
structures is more worthwhile than the hope of
"truth." Discusses several novels suitable for use
in a philosophy class: Heinlein's Space Cadet,
Leiber's own Beyond Rejection and The Big Time, and
Russ's The Female Man. (JS)

D20   Magill, Frank N., ed. Science Fiction: Alien
        Encounter. Pasadena, CA: Salem Softbacks, 1981 pbk.
        Essays on seventy-five science fiction works that
        deal with the theme of alien encounter. Each essay
        offers publication information, a list of principle
        characters, and a 2,000-word analysis. Reprinted
        from Survey of Science Fiction Literature (Salem
        Press, 1979). (MBT)

D21   Merritt, James D. "She Pluck'd, She Eat." In
        Future Females. Ed. Marleen S. Barr. Bowling
        Green, OH: Bowling Green State Univ. Popular Press,
        1981, pp. 37-41.
        Discusses the theme of sinful Eve in C. S.
        Lewis's Perelandra, H. P. Lovecraft's The Dunwich
        Horror, and Carolyn Neeper's A Place Beyond Man.
        (TPD)

D22   Pearson, Carol. "Coming Home: Four Feminist Utopias
        and Patriarchal Experience." In Future Females.
        Ed. Marleen S. Barr. Bowling Green, OH: Bowling
        Green State Univ. Popular Press, 1981, pp. 63-70.
        The sexually equalitarian societies of four
        novels are presented as offering to their respective
        narrators a nurturing, liberating environment: Mary
        Bradley Lane's Mizora: A Prophesy, Charlotte Perkins
        Gilman's Herland, Dorothy Bryant's The Kin of Ata
        Are Waiting for You, and Mary Staton's The Legend of
        Biel. (TPD)

D23   Rabkin, Eric S. "Science Fiction Women Before
        Liberation." In Future Females. Ed. Marleen S.
        Barr. Bowling Green, OH: Bowling Green State Univ.
        Popular Press, 1981, pp. 9-25.
        Earlier science fiction maltreated women in many
        ways but mostly by ignoring them, and the situation
        is not yet fully remedied. (TPD)

D24   Russ, Joanna. "Recent Feminist Utopias." In Future
        Females. Ed. Marleen S. Barr. Bowling Green, OH:
        Bowling Green State Univ. Popular Press, 1981, pp.
        71-87.
        Ten works published in the 1970s present remark-
        ably similar pictures of feminist utopias. Con-
        siders works by Monique Wittig, Suzy McKee Charnas,
        Ursula Le Guin, Joanna Russ, Samuel Delany, Marion
        Zimmer Bradley, Marge Piercy, Sally Gearhart,
        Catherine Madsen, and Alice Sheldon. (TPD)

D25   Sanders, Scott. "Women as Nature in Science Fic-
        tion." In Future Females. Ed. Marleen S. Barr.

Bowling Green, OH: Bowling Green State Univ. Popular
Press, 1981, pp. 42-59.
   In the largely male-centered genre of science
fiction, women are generally perceived as myster-
ious, irrational, instinctive, fertile, and mind-
less--all characteristics commonly associated with
nature. (TPD)

D26   Sargent, Lyman Tower. "An Ambiguous Legacy: The
      Role and Position of Women in the English Utopia."
      In Future Females. Ed. Marleen S. Barr. Bowling
      Green, OH: Bowling Green State Univ. Popular Press,
      1981, pp. 88-99.
         Sargent surveys many eutopias (good places) but
      finds little interest in genuine reform of women's
      position in society. (TPD)

D27   Stableford, Brian. "Man-Made Catastrophes in SF."
      Foundation, No. 22 (1981), pp. 56-85.
         A wide-ranging discussion stretching back to the
      beginnings of literature and focusing on many recent
      science fiction works on the theme of catastrophe,
      in particular imagined disasters caused by human
      agency. (DMH)

D28   Tracy, Ann B. The Gothic Novel 1790-1830: Plot
      Summaries and Index to Motifs. Lexington, KY:
      University Press of Kentucky, 1981.
         Contains plot summaries arranged by author of two
      hundred novels published during the period. Useful
      for its detailed motif index and index of charcters.
      (MBT)

D29   Vampires [cassette]. Washington, D.C.: National
      Public Radio, 1978.
         Readings, sound effects, and monologues by ex-
      perts who examine the old and new of ancient vampire
      legends. (AT)

D30   Wagner, Karl Edward. "On Fantasy: 'Even a Man Who
      Is Pure in Heart.'" FN, No. 38 (1981), pp. 5-7, 31.
         Survey of werewolf novels, pondering why that
      monster hasn't inspired a "classic" tale on the
      level of Dracula. (JS)

D31   Whitehurst, Carol A. "Images of the Sexes in Sci-
      ence Fiction." International Journal of Women's
      Studies, 3 (1980), 327-37.
         A content analysis of twenty-six Hugo-winning
      novels (1953-1979) reveals that science fiction,
      even with its capacity to deal with any imagined
      society, has lagged behind actual changes in
      female-male relationships and roles. Presents data
      on visibility of women characters, occupation,
      education, age, marital status and parenthood,
      revealing how men and women are stereotyped. (JAG)

E. Collective Author Studies

E01   Anderson, Katherine Ann Thomen. "Christian Concepts and Doctrines in Selected Works of Science Fiction." Ph.D. dissertation, University of Denver, 1981; DAI, 42: 4829A.
      Examines Walter M. Miller, Jr.'s A Canticle for Leibowitz; Frank Herbert's Dune, Dune Messiah, and Children of Dune; and C.S. Lewis' Out of the Silent Planet, Perelandra, and That Hideous Strength as science fiction works which impact on Christian values. The author concludes that while Lewis and Miller celebrate Christian concepts, Herbert's trilogy shows them as false and unnecessary, focusing instead on the power of the individual. (PA)

E02   Brigg, Peter. "Frank Herbert and Bill Ransom's The Jesus Incident: Variations on the Godgame." PS, 1 (March 1981), 26-34.
      Compares this work to John Fowles's The Magus, as a work more successful in using religious concepts such as free will vs. manipulation by "gods." The Herbert-Ransom novel is too crowded with ideas and interpretations to do justice to its major theme. (JS)

E03   Carpenter, Humphrey. The Inklings: J. R. R. Tolkien, C. S. Lewis, Charles Williams, and Their Friends. New York: Ballantine, 1981 pbk.
      A reprint of Carpenter's 1978 book, the first collective biography of these remarkable friends and scholars, the Inklings. Attempts to show how the ideas and interests of the group contrasted sharply with the general intellectual and literary spirit of the 1920s and 1930s. The focus is on C. S. Lewis, to whom the Inklings owed their existence as a group. (MBT)

E04   Christopher, Joe R. "An Inklings Bibliography (15)." Mythlore, No. 26 (1981), pp. 42-46.
      Annotated bibliography of books or articles that deal with the writers--or even mention them in passing. (JS)

E05   -------. "An Inklings Bibliography (16)." Mythlore, No. 27 (1981), pp. 43-47.
      See annotation above.

E06   -------. "An Inklings Bibliography (17)."
       Mythlore, No. 28 (1981), pp. 43-47.
          See annotation E04.

E07   -------. "An Inklings Bibliography (18)."
       Mythlore, No. 29 (1981), pp. 43-47.
          See annotation E04.

E08   Elliot, Jeffrey M. The Future of the Space Program:
       Large Corporations & Society. Interviews with 22
       Science-Fiction Writers. San Bernardino, CA: Borgo
       Press, 1981.
          The writers have prepared short essays in re-
       sponse to questions on the U.S. space program and on
       corporate planning for society's future. Also
       issued in paperback. [Contents not annotated.]
       (MBT)

E09   Erlich, Richard D. "A Womb with a View: Domesticat-
       ing the Fantastic in Pohl and Kornbluth's Gladiator-
       at-Law." Foundation, No. 23 (1981), pp. 31-39.
          An argument that this 1955 satiric novel makes
       use of elements that "we usually think of as the
       fantastic." (DMH)

E10   Ferguson, Mary Louise Dechert. "My Spectre Around
       Me: The Reluctant Rebellion of the Gothic Novel-
       ists." Ph.D. dissertation, Vanderbilt University,
       1981; DAI, 42: 4457A.
          The world of the early Gothic writers was filled
       with violence and revolution, a bloody pattern
       paralleled in their fiction. The writers, propelled
       by their fear which generated their age, used this
       genre as a veil against harsh realities by trans-
       ferring them into fastastic fiction. Includes a
       discussion of Shelley's Frankenstein. (PA)

E11   Fitzgerald, Dorothy Hobson. "Theories of Joy and
       Substitution in the Works of C. S. Lewis and Charles
       Williams." CSL, 12 (January 1981), 1-8.
          Examines the depiction of the use and misuse of
       power in Williams' Descent into Hell and Lewis' Till
       We Have Faces. (JAG)

E12   Greenberg, Martin H. ed. Fantastic Lives: Auto-
       biographical Essays by Notable Science Fiction
       Writers. Alternatives series. Carbondale: Southern
       Illinois Univ. Press, 1981.
          A collection of original autobiographical essays
       by Harlan Ellison, Philip Jose Farmer, R. A.
       Lafferty, Katherine MacLean, Barry N. Malzberg, Mack
       Reynolds, Margaret St. Clair, Norman Spinrad, and A.
       E. van Vogt. A bibliography of the author's major
       works follows each essay. [See under names of
       individual writers in Section F.] (TPD)

E13   Grigsby, John L. "Asimov's Foundation Trilogy and
       Herbert's Dune Trilogy: A Vision Reversed." SFS, 8
       (1981), 149-55.

Despite their mutual dislike of the other's trilogy, as documented in this essay, Herbert utilized many of Asimov's specific ideas and techniques in reversing Asimov's vision of the future. (DMH)

E14   Hamilton, Elissa L. A. "The Muse As Pilgrim: SF Imagery in the Poetry of Diane Wakoski, Margaret Atwood, Marge Piercy." _Starline_, 5 (March/April 1981), 19-25.
Part 1 of a lengthy study, supported by many quotations, from three leading feminist poets. The role of metaphor, monster, cybernetics, and much else is explained. (TWH)

E15   Kotzin, Michael C. "C. S. Lewis and George Mac-Donald: _The Silver Chair_ and the Princess Books." _Mythlore_, No. 27 (1981). pp. 5-15.
Compares plot and other features of _The Silver Chair_ and the two Princess books. Overall, the two writers are alike in creating Christian fairy tales, reminding their audience of reality/value beyond the familiar world. (JS)

E16   Limon, John Keith. "Imagining Science: The Influence and Metamorphosis of Science in Charles Brockden Brown, Edgar Allan Poe, and Nathaniel Hawthorne." Ph.D. dissertation, University of California, Berkeley, 1981; _DAI_, 42: 5122A.
During the decades in which Brown, Poe, and Hawthorne wrote, science grew in intellectual prestige and became quite complex in its philosophy; thus writers found themselves in an intellectual world they only partially understood. Through an analysis of their works this thesis casts these three authors as examples of the artist as "half-intellectual." (PA)

- E17   Meikle, Jeffrey L. "Other Frequencies: The Parallel Worlds of Thomas Pynchon and H. P. Lovecraft." _Modern Fiction Studies_, 27 (1981), 287-94.
Demonstrates the parallels between Pynchon's novel _The Crying of Lot 49_ and Lovecraft's horror classic _The Call of Cthulhu_. (PA)

E18   Mendelson. Michael Todd. "The Modernization of Prose Romance: The Radical Form of William Morris and George MacDonald." Ph.D. dissertation, Washington State University, 1981; _DAI_, 42: 4460A.
Radicalized romance as a genre moves in the direction of myth and customarily involves an "other-world" journey beyond boundaries of ordinary existence. (PA)

E19   Mosig, Dirk W. "Poe, Hawthorne, and Lovecraft: Variations on a Scene of Panic." _The Romantist_, No. 4-5 (1980-81), pp. 43-44.
Traces the influence upon Lovecraft's 1921 tale "The Outsider" by Poe's "The Masque of the Red

Death" and "William Wilson" and Hawthorne's "Journal
of a Solitary Man." Contrasts each writer's evo-
cation of the panic emotion in crown scenes. (SE)

E20   Parrinder, Patrick. "Siblings in Space: The Science
       Fiction of J. B. S. Haldane and Naomi Mitchison."
       Foundation, No. 22 (1981), pp. 49-56.
           A review of the work of these two writers,
       brother and sister, the one (J. B. S.) labeled "one
       of the great debunkers of his age" and the other
       called a writer who maintained a sceptical "lovehate
       relation" with science all during her writing.
       (DMH)

E21   Pauline, Sister CSM. "Secondary Worlds: Lewis and
       Tolkien." CSL, 12 (May 1981), 1-8.
           Compares the degree of detail in the creation of
       Tolkien's Middle Earth with that in Lewis' Narnia in
       the light of Tolkien's comment that Narnia is inad-
       equately developed in detail. The essay asserts
       that Lewis' settings are not carelessly undetailed
       but purposeful: in Narnia setting is secondary to
       message. (JAG)

E22   Ratcliff, John D. "She and Tolkien." Mythlore, No.
       28 (1981), pp. 6-8.
           A comparison of She and Galadriel, Kor and
       Gondolin, to show Haggard's influence on Tolkien.
       (JS)

E23   Schweitzer, Darrell. "Edmond Hamilton and Leigh
       Brackett." In Science Fiction Voices #5. Ed.
       Darrell Schweitzer. San Bernardino, CA: Borgo
       Press, 1981, pp. 35-40.
           Hamilton and Brackett recall the times and cir-
       cumstances in which they began their careers in
       science fiction. (JME)

E24   -------. Science Fiction Voices #5. San
       Bernardino, CA: Borgo Press, 1981.
           Interviews with nine science fiction and fantasy
       writers, including Isaac Asimov, Leigh Brackett, Lin
       Carter, Lester del Rey, Edmond Hamilton, Frank
       Belknap Long, Clifford Simak, Wilson Tucker, and
       Jack Williamson. Also issued in paperback. [Each
       interview is separately annotated in Section F; see
       also E23.] (JME)

E25   Stableford, Brian M. "Edmond Hamilton and Leigh
       Brackett: An Appreciation." In Masters of Science
       Fiction: Essays on Six Science Fiction Writers. Ed.
       Brian M. Stableford. San Bernardino CA: Borgo
       Press, 1981, pp. 6-14.
           Stableford contends that the two writers do not
       belong to the science fiction of today. Rather,
       their work reflects the world that inspired it--
       namely, the 1920s and 1930s. (JME)

E26   -------. Masters of Science Fiction: Essays on Six
Science Fiction Writers. San Bernardino, CA: Borgo
Press, 1981.
    This volume brings together five essays on the
life and work of six science fiction writers--
authors whose writing Stableford has found interest-
ing and entertaining: Edmond Hamilton, Leigh Brackett, Barry N. Malzberg, Kurt Vonnegut, Robert
Silverberg, and Mack Reynolds. Also issued in
paperback. [Each essay is separately annotated in
Section F; see also E25.] (JME)

E27   Tritt, Michael. "Byron's 'Darkness' and Asimov's
'Nightfall.'" SFS, 8 (1981), 26-28.
    Byron's 1816 poem and Asimov's story share the
same vision and apply it to man in a similar way.
Tritt suggests Byron as a source though Asimov does
not explicitly acknowledge the debt. (DMH)

E28   Zahorski, Kenneth J., and Robert H. Boyer. Lloyd
Alexander, Evangeline Walton Ensley, Kenneth Morris:
A Primary and Secondary Bibliography. Masters of
Science Fiction and Fantasy. Boston: G. K. Hall,
1981.
    Provides comprehensive checklists of fiction and
nonfiction by these three writers published in books
and periodicals, with annotated listings of secondary material. Includes informative biograph-
ical/critical essays thematically linking the
writers by their use of the Mabinogion, a classic of
Welsh literature which provided inspiration and the
direct source for their major literary contributions. (MBT)

F. Individual Author Studies

BRIAN W. ALDISS (See also C01, C02, C34)

F01   Milicia, Joseph, introd. Starswarm. By Brian W.
       Aldiss. Boston: Gregg Press, 1978.
            The stories of Starswarm "dramatize the tensions
       between freedom and constraint, capability and
       limitation." (AT)

F02   Spinrad, Norman, introd. Galaxies Like Grains of
       Sand. By Brian W. Aldiss. Boston: Gregg Press,
       1977.
            Argues that because Galaxies is concerned with
       time and evolution it can be seen as a survey of
       Aldiss' subsequent career. (AT)

LLOYD ALEXANDER (See E28)

CHESTER ANDERSON

F03   Williams, Paul, introd. The Butterfly Kid. By
       Chester Anderson. Boston: Gregg Press, 1977.
            How the work demonstrates the connection between
       science fiction and the hippie movement of the late
       1960s. (AT)

POUL ANDERSON

F04   Anderson, Poul, introd. The Byworlder. By Poul
       Anderson. Boston: Gregg Press, 1978.
            The future is predicted in The Byworlder as a
       result of Anderson's reflection upon the world
       around him in Berkeley, California, c. 1969-70.
       (AT)

F05   -------, introd. The Horn of Time. By Poul
       Anderson. Boston: Gregg Press, 1978.
            A brief discussion of sources of short stories in
       this collection. (AT)

F06   -------, introd. The Long Way Home. By Poul
       Anderson. Boston: Gregg Press, 1978.
            A historical footnote to The Long Way Home,
       noting John W. Campbell's interest in the proslavery
       aspects of the novel, which resulted in several
       stories written with that point of view. (AT)

F07   -------, introd. <u>The Night Face and Other Stories</u>.
       By Poul Anderson. Boston: Gregg Press, 1978.
           Though the four stories in this collection are
       part of Anderson's Technic Civilization series, they
       are peripheral to the narrative of the other works
       and have no precise analogies in the actual past.
       (AT)

F08   -------, introd. <u>Orbit Unlimited</u>. By Poul
       Anderson. Boston: Gregg Press, 1978.
           Anderson discusses his research to create the
       planet Rustum and asserts that in writing the book
       he "wanted to utter a word for freedom."

F09   -------, introd. <u>Two Worlds</u>. By Poul Anderson.
       Boston: Gregg Press, 1978.
           A brief observation that future history requires
       knowledge of the present and the past and illus-
       tration of the correct and incorrect aspects of
       Heinlein's "Solution Unsatisfactory." (AT)

F10   Brenner, Malcolm. "Interview: Poul Anderson."
       <u>Future Life</u>, No. 104 (1981), pp. 26-28.
           Anderson discusses his approach to art and sci-
       ence. (MBT)

F11   Miesel, Sandra, introd. <u>The People of the Wind</u>. By
       Poul Anderson. Boston: Gregg Press, 1977.
           Miesel places this novel in Anderson's Technic
       Civilization series and demonstrates its development
       of the theme of conflicts in a society composed of
       both humans and nonhumans. (AT)

       ISAAC ASIMOV (See also B02, B03, B04, D13, E13, E27,
       I01)

F12   Gentle, Mary. "Bright Walls of the Universe."
       <u>Vector</u>, No. 104 (1981), pp. 15-17.
           Reassesses "Nightfall" and questions its classic
       status, claiming that it is wholly within the pulp
       traditions with cardboard characters and all the
       social conventions of mid-twentieth-century America.
       Reveals flaws in the story and bad writing but
       maintains that it nonetheless creates a powerful
       apocalyptic vision. (JF)

F13   Hood, Susan. "Isaac Asimov: The Great Explainer."
       <u>Instructor</u>, 90 (February 1981), 32-35.
           Deeply concerned about learning, Asimov comments
       on TV as a stimulator for reading; science fiction
       as a way of capturing children's interest as well as
       helping them become accustomed to the idea of
       change; and the future of education in a comput-
       erized world. (PA)

F14   Hull, Elizabeth Anne. "The Little Professor, Intu-
       itionist: A Transactional Analysis of Isaac Asimov's
       <u>The Gods Themselves</u>." <u>Extrapolation</u>, 22 (1981).
       146-54.

In Asimov's attempt to create aliens who are at
once truly different from humans but ultimately
accessible to readers, he unknowingly echoes Eric
Berne's theory of personality structure, "transac-
tional analysis." Thus his fiction is a liberating
experience for readers caught in narrow roles. (JS)

F15   Lackey, Douglas P. "Logic and Ethics of Asimovian
       Reality Changes." PS, 1 (March 1981), 35-40.
          Delighted with The End of Eternity for its medi-
       tations on time travel as a "complex, looped, and
       voluntary" process. (JS)

F16   Schweitzer, Darrell. "Isaac Asimov." In Science
       Fiction Voices #5. Ed. Darrell Schweitzer. San
       Bernardino, CA: Borgo Press, 1981 pp. 7-14.
          In this interview, Asimov explores the topic of
       space travel, its depiction in science fiction,
       predictions concerning its feasibility, colonization
       of the planets, and the scientific feasibility of
       science fiction as it relates to these topics. He
       also discusses his career and working philosophy.
       (JME)

F17   Warrick, Patricia S. "The Contrapuntal Design of
       Artificial Evolution in Asimov's 'The Bicentennial
       Man.'" Extrapolation, 22 (1981), 231-41.
          This story is the culmination of Asimov's long
       fascination with robots/limits of man and his ma-
       chines, as it shows machine accepting the limitation
       of mortality in order to become "human." (JS)

       MARGARET ATWOOD (See E14)

       BARRINGTON J. BAYLEY (See B05, D13)

       PETER S. BEAGLE (See C26)

       EDWARD BELLAMY (See F63, F261)

       GREGORY BENFORD

F18   Benford, Gregory. "A String of Days." SFR, No. 38
       (1981), pp. 14-20.
          This article--in the form of a journal--covers
       the period May 8-June 3, 1980. In it, Benford
       provides the reader with a fascinating insight into
       the mind and work of one of the field's most cele-
       brated talents. (JME)

F19   Cassutt, Michael. "Interview: Gregory Benford."
       Future Life, No. 24 (1981), pp. 40-42.
          An interview with a physicist who writes truly
       scientific science fiction. (MBT)

       ROBERT HUGH BENSON

F20   O'Meara, Thomas F. "Catholic Science Fiction,
       1900." America, 144 (1981), 525-27.

In 1900 Roman Catholic priest Benson wrote a
science fiction novel, Lord of the World, in which
he depicted events as he thought they would be one
hundred years hence. This essay discusses the
theological implications of the work. (PA)

OLES BERDNYK

F21   Smyrniw, Walter. "The Theme of Man-godhood in Oles
Berdnyk's Science Fiction." Journal of Ukrainian
Studies, 6 (Spring 1981), 3-19.
       Discusses the entire range of Berdnyk's fiction
from its early concerns with adventure and mechani-
zation to its more mystical final phase which con-
centrated on the possibilities for man's psychic
evolution. (TPD)

MICHAEL BISHOP (SEE E27)

ALGERNON BLACKWOOD

F22   Columbo, John Robert. Blackwood's Books: A
Bibliography Devoted to Algernon Blackwood.
Toronto: Hounslow Press, 1981 pbk.
       The first bibliography of the works of the noted
British author of supernatural and weird fiction.
Documents English-language first editions and most
impressions, reprints, and new editions. (But an
occasional first edition is not documented if
unavailable for examination.) Seven appendixes
provided allied information about the man and his
work. (MBT)

F23   Reaver, J. Russell. "From Seed to Fruit: The
Doubling of Psychic Landscape in Algernon Blackwood's The Centaur." The Romantist, No. 4-5 (1980-
81), pp. 55-58.
       Studies Blackwood's novel with the aid of psycho-
logical theories in Lyall Watson's Lifetide: The
Biology of the Unconscious (1979). (SE)

JAMES BLISH (See D06, D07)

ROBERT BLOCH

F24   Collins, Tom. "Robert Bloch: Society as Insane
Asylum." TZM, No. 4 (1981), pp. 13-17.
       An interview with the popular horror writer,
stressing the inspiration for the film Psycho and
details of its filming. Also discusses his science
fiction novel, This Crowded Earth (1968) and Bloch's
views on horror in the films. (SE)

BEN BOVA (See also B07, I02)

F25   "Rigel Interviews Ben Bova." Rigel Science Fiction
(Summer 1981), pp. 19-23, 31.
       Bova talks about his science fiction writing and

work as an editor. Explains his views on contemporary novels and film,and on the court case he and
Harlan Ellison won against Paramount. (TWH)

LEIGH BRACKETT (See E23, E25)

RAY BRADBURY (See also D06)

F26   Bishop, Michael. "Pitching Pennies Against the
       Starboard Bulkhead: A Reverie for Mister Ray."
       Thrust, No. 17 (1981), pp. 14-17.
          Bishop discusses his introduction to Bradbury's A
       Medicine for Melancholy, and the influence the book
       had then and continues to have on his life and work.
       Bishop then examines several of Bradbury's most
       famous works, among which are The Martian Chroni-
       cles, The October Country, The Illulstrated Man, I
       Sing the Body Electric, and Dandelion Wine. (JME)

F27   DeArmond, William Duncan, Jr. "Ray Bradbury and
       Oral Interpretation: An Interpreters Theatre Adap-
       tation of Fahrenheit 451." Ph.D. dissertation,
       Southern Illinois University at Carbondale, 1981;
       DAI, 42: 4197A.
          Addresses the problem of oral interpretation of
       speculative fiction and specifically the works of
       Bradbury. Through an examination of Fahrenheit 451,
       this dissertation shows how the novel's thematic
       levels and narrative stance are translated from the
       printed page to interpreter's stage in both film and
       theater. (PA)

F28   Linkfield, Thomas P. "The Fiction of Ray Bradbury:
       Universal Themes in Midwestern Settings." Mid-
       western Miscellany, 8 (1980), 44-101.
          Examines Bradbury's development of the themes of
       the stasis versus change, the fear of death and
       darkness, and the need to accept reality in his
       novels with nostalgic midwestern settings: The
       Halloween Man, Something Wicked This Way Comes, and
       Dandelion Wine. (JAG)

F29   Plank, Robert. "The Expedition to the Planet of
       Paranoia." Extrapolation, 22 (1981), 171-85.
          Begins with an analysis of "April 2000: The Third
       Expedition" (aka "Mars Is Heaven") from Bradbury's
       The Martian Chronicles, showing the shift from
       unthinking joy at the supposedly resurrected dead to
       the horrible revelation that masquerading Martians
       are waiting to kill humans, to odd coda as Martians
       bury dead humans. Explains story as a regression to
       childhood (idealized version of irresponsible exis-
       tence) that is punished during return to reality.
       (JS)

F30   Touponce, William Ferdinand. "Ray Bradbury and the
       Poetics of Reverie: A Study of Fantasy, Science
       Fiction, and The Reading Progress." Ph.D. disser

tation, University of Massachusetts, 1981; <u>DAI</u>, 41: 5093A.
    The role of the teacher in the fantastic fiction of Bradbury, an author whose stories enable his audience to imaginatively transform the narrative event. (PA)

MARION ZIMMER BRADLEY (See also D24)

F31   Bradley, Marion Zimmer, introd. <u>The Bloody Sun and "To Keep the Oath</u>." By Marion Zimmer Bradley. Boston: Gregg Press, 1979.
      Bradley explains how all the elements of the Darkover series are put together in <u>The Bloody Sun</u>. (AT)

F32   -------, introd. <u>The Shattered Chain</u>. By Marion Zimmer Bradley. Boston: Gregg Press, 1979.
      Recounts feminist reaction to the Free Amazons in the novel and Bradley's response that her characters, and all people, are free to choose their own chains or choose the illusion of freedom. (AT)

F33   -------, introd. <u>Star of Danger</u>. By Marion Zimmer Bradley. Boston: Gregg Press, 1979.
      Discusses the ways writers get and use ideas and the genesis of <u>Star of Danger</u>. (AT)

F34   -------, introd. <u>Stormqueen!</u> By Marion Zimmer Bradley. Boston: Gregg Press, 1979.
      Recounts the genesis of <u>Stormqueen!</u> and demonstrates where it fits in the Darkover series; argues that all her heroines assert themselves in a heterosexual society. (AT)

F35   -------, introd. <u>The Winds of Darkover</u>. By Marion Zimmer Bradley. Boston: Gregg Press, 1979.
      <u>The Winds of Darkover</u> is regarded as the book that got the Darkover series off the ground, and it is Bradley's first book with a female protagonist. (AT)

F36   -------, introd. <u>The World Wreckers</u>. By Marion Zimmer Bradley. Boston: Gregg Press, 1979.
      Bradley explains the origins of the dually-sexed Chieri in the novel and the influence of Le Guin's <u>The Left Hand of Darkness</u> and David Gerrold and Larry Niven's <u>The Flying Sorcerers</u> on the plot of her novel. (AT)

F37   Schwartz, Susan M. "Other Worlds: By the Light of the Bloody Sun." <u>FN</u>, No. 32 (1981), pp. 12-15.
      Personal memories of reading Bradley's Darkover novels, plus summary-critique of the novels. (JS)

F38   Sturgeon, Theodore, introd. <u>Darkover Landfall</u>. By Marion Zimmer Bradley. Boston: Gregg Press, 1978.
      Sturgeon reminisces about his first encounter

with Bradley and asserts that she excels in describing not only the world of Darkover but also the
personal interactions of her characters. (AT)

JOHANNA AND GUNTHER BRAUN

F39   Suvin, Darko. "Playful Cognizing, or Technical
       Errors in Harmonyville: The Science Fiction of
       Johanna and Gunther Braun." SFS, 8 (1981), 72-79.
          A pioneering discussion of four works by an East
       German married couple who publish all their works
       together; Suvin finds revolutionary themes and irony
       similar to Stanislaw Lem's. (DMH)

CHARLES BROCKDEN BROWN (see E16)

F40   Christophersen, Bill. "Charles Brockden Brown's
       Ormond: The Secret Witness as Ironic Motif." Modern
       Language Studies, 10 (1980), 37-41.
          The motif of the "secret witness" is an ironic
       metaphor of initiation into the recognition of evil.
       (JAG)

F41   Levin, Robert S. "Villainy and the Fear of Con-
       spiracy in Charles Brockden Brown's Ormond." Early
       American Literature, 15 (1980), 124-40.
          Examines Ormond as a figure embodying the late
       eighteenth-century American fear of conspiracy and
       conspiratorial groups, especially the Illuminati.
       (JAG)

F42   Mohanahan, Kathleen Nolan. "The Relationship Be-
       tween Character and Idea in the Novels of Charles
       Brockden Brown." Ph.D. dissertation, New York
       University, 1981; DAI, 42: 3159A.
          Focuses on four conditions--isolation, search,
       crisis, and contemplation--which recur in the his-
       tories of Brown's characters. (PA)

F43   Rosenthal, Bernard [ed.] Critical Essays on Charles
       Brockden Brown. Critical Essays on American Litera-
       ture. Boston: G. K. Hall, 1981.
          An anthology of reprinted reviews and early
       criticism, plus eight original essays and a
       comprehensive bibliography of criticism on Brown
       [Contents not annotated.] (MBT)

F44   Yarbrough, Stephen R. "The Tragedy of Isolation:
       Fictional Technique and Environmentalism in
       Wieland." Studies in American Fiction, 8 (1980),
       98-105.
          Examines Wieland as a study of the tragic effects
       of emotional and intellectual isolation on the
       character of the narrator, Clara, whose isolation is
       a result of her lack of education and involvement
       with society. (JAG)

FREDRIC BROWN

F45   Baird, Newton. A Key to Fredric Brown's Wonderland:
       A Study and An Annotated Bibliographical Checklist.
       Georgetown, CA: Talisman Literary Research, 1981
       pbk.
           Contains a study, chronology, and annotated
       bibliography, plus reminiscences by Brown's wife and
       his agent. Includes an appendix, subject, author,
       and title index. Illustrated. (MBT)

JOHN BRUNNER (See C13, D07)

ALGIS BUDRYS (See also I03, F62)

F46   Budrys, Algis, introd. Rogue Moon. By Algis
       Budrys. Boston: Gregg Press, 1977.
           The author reveals that he wrote The Death Ma-
       chine (original title) to be "the SF story of love
       as the only effective adversary of death." (AT)

F47   Milicia, Joseph, introd. Rogue Moon. By Algis
       Budrys. Boston: Gregg Press, 1977.
           Compares the novel version to the novella and
       praises the novel both as a character study of the
       scientist Edward Hawks and as a successful combi-
       nation of two common science fiction subjects: the
       matter transmitter and the exploration of an alien
       environment. (AT)

ANTHONY BURGESS

F48   Brewer, Jeutonne. Anthony Burgess: A Bibliography.
       Scarecrow Author Bibliographies, No. 47. Metuchen,
       NJ and London: Scarecrow Press, 1980.
           This bibliograhy reflects the increasing critical
       interest in Anthony Burgess and his works. Nine
       alphabetically-arranged sections contain material by
       Burgess: novels, short stories, poems, nonfiction
       books and sections of books, works translated, works
       edited, articles, essays and reviews, interviews,
       and recordings. Four alphabetically-arranged
       sections contain materials about Burgess: books and
       sections of books, dissertations, articles and es-
       says, and bibliographies. Extensive annotations
       provide information about the scope of Burgess' in-
       terests in the areas of literature, language, and
       music. Three indexes provide access to the biblio-
       graphy by author and title, and by names and titles
       mentioned in the works by Burgess. The most com-
       prehensive source of information available for
       Burgess and his works. (MBT)

EDGAR RICE BURROUGHS

F49   Farmer, Philip Jose. Tarzan Alive. New York:
       Playboy, 1981 pbk.
           A minutely detailed and documented research into

the life of "a living person." Asserts that Tarzan
not only lived (and lives), but that he is related
to other equally "real" people, notably Sherlock
Holmes. Depicts Lord Greystoke as immortal, and, in
the best tradition of the Baker Street Irregulars,
manages to deify its principal beyond even the
popular myths. A complex, outrageously-scaled
spoof. Reprint of the 1972 Doubleday edition, orig-
inally titled Tarzan Alive: A Definitive Biography
of Lord Greystoke. (MBT)

F50   Holtsmark, Erling B. Tarzan and Tradition: Clas-
sical Myth in Popular Culture. Contributions to the
Study of Popular Culture, No. 1. Westport, CT:
Greenwood Press, 1981.
       A study of Burroughs' first six Tarzan books
(Tarzan of the Apes, The Return of Tarzan, The
Beasts of Tarzan, The Son of Tarzan, Tarzan and the
Jewels of Opar, and Jungle Tales of Tarzan) which
reveals parallels between Tarzan's story ad the
heroic sagas of ancient Greece and Rome. Holtsmark
explores the classical relationships evident in
Burroughs' language and narrative style, and finds
Tarzan himself to be a surprisingly complex literary
persona whose roots in the mythical heroes of antiq-
uity, notably Odysseus, are combined with features
borrowed from American Indian traditions. The
author also explores the erotic and Darwinian elements in Burroughs' thematic structure. Secondary
bibliography. (MBT)

ITALO CALVINO (See also C26)

F51   Cannon, Joann. "Literary Signification: An Analysis
of Calvino's Trilogy." Symposium, 34 (Spring 1981),
3-12.
       The Italian author uses the fantastic element in
his trilogy Il visconte dimezzato, Il barone
rampante, and Il cavaliere inesistente, to demon-
strate his deep feelings about the relationship
between fiction and reality. (PA)

RAMSEY CAMPBELL

F52   [Reeder, Dave.] "The Mythos Writers: Ramsey
Campbell." Fantasy Macabre, No. 2 (1981), pp. 4-7.
       An interview with this important British weird
horror author. Emphasis is on his interest in
Lovecraft and the so-called "Mythos" (Yog-Sothoth
myth-cycle). (SE)

KAREL CAPEK

F53   Harkins, William E., introd. The Absolute at Large.
By Karel Capek. Westport, CT: Hyperion Press, 1974.
       Demonstrates that this satiric comedy embodies
the central idea of of Capek's works on science
themes--his mistrust of all absolutes. (AT)

LIN CARTER

F54   Schweitzer, Darrell. "Lin Carter.: In Science
       Fiction Voices #5. Ed. Darrell Schweitzer. San
       Bernardino, CA: Borgo Press, 1981, pp. 14-26.
           Lin Carter recalls his editorial beginnings, his
       initial tastes in fantasy, and his early involvement
       in the fantasy field. He also talks about the craft
       of writing. (JME)

CARLOS CASTANEDA (See C16)

ROBERT W. CHAMBERS

F55   Moskowitz, Sam. "The Light Fantastics of Robert W.
       Chambers." Introd. In Search of the Unknown. By
       Robert W. Chambers. Westport, CT: Hyperion Press,
       1974.
           Demonstrates Chambers' influence on science
       fiction and fantasy and chronicles the publishing
       history of In Search of the Unknown while noting
       similar stories published contemporaneously. (AT)

SUZY McKEE CHARNAS (See also D24)

F56   Charnas, Suzy McKee. "A Woman Appeared." In Future
       Females. Ed. Marleen S. Barr. Bowling Green, OH:
       Bowling Green State Univ. Popular Press, 1981, pp.
       103-08.
           As Charnas' feminist consciousness developed in
       the early 1970s, she found herself moving her pro-
       tagonist, Alldera, closer to the heart of her first
       science fiction
       novel, Walk to the End of the World. (TPD)

G. K. CHESTERTON (See also C18)

F57   Grist, Anthony. "Chesterton and the Decadence."
       The Chesterton Review, 7 (1981), 250-57.
           A survey of the influence of the decadence and
       diabolism of the 1890s on Chesterton's thinking and
       art. (RCS)

F58   Leigh, David J. "Politics and Perspective in The
       Man Who Was Thursday." The Chesterton Review, 7
       (1981), 329-36.
           An analysis of The Man Who Was Thursday via an
       interconnected pattern of three allegories: the
       approach to the Ultimate, the revelation of the
       nature of the Ultimate, and the socio-political
       implications of the first two. (RCS)

F59   Sullivan, John. "Additions to Chesterton Three."
       The Chesterton Review, 7 (1981), 225-28.
           An addendum to Sullivan's ongoing bibliography of
       Chesterton, which began with Chesterton: A Biblio-
       graphy (1958) and Chesterton Continued (1968).
       (RCS)

CATHERINE ANTHONY CLARK (See C31)

HAL CLEMENT

F60   Hassler, Donald M.   "The Hard Science Fiction of Hal
       Clement."   The Gamut, No. 3 (Spring/Summer 1981),
       pp. 46-54.
          Clement, Hassler argues, is one of the finest
       writers of hard science fiction and "often reveals
       in his work a complexity of theme, an intricacy and
       appropriateness of tonal effect, and an overall
       significance that are characteristic of [science
       fiction] at its best." (TPD)

PAUL COLLINS

F61   Ikin, Van. "The Paul Collins Interview." Science
       Fiction, 3 (1981), 57-63.
          An interview with the writer, editor, and pub-
       lisher followed by a checklist of stories by
       Collins. (DMH)

D. G. COMPTON

F62   Budrys, Algis, introd. Synthajoy. By D. G.
       Compton. Boston: Gregg Press, 1977.
          Relates the history of mind control experimenta-
       tion in reality and in science fiction, and praises
       Compton's characterization of Thea Cadence as a
       fully-realized woman. (AT)

WILLIAM WALLACE COOK

F63   Moskowitz, Sam. "Cook's Tour of Tomorrow." Introd.
       A Round Trip to the Year 2000. By William Wallace
       Cook. Westport, CT: Hyperion Press, 1974.
          Argues that Cook's science fiction was influenced
       by The Time Machine and by Looking Backward and that
       it is lifted above hack writing by its social criti-
       cism and satire. (AT)

SUSAN COOPER (See C31)

JUANITA COULSON

F64   Elliot, Jeffrey. "Interview: Juanita Coulson." FN,
       No. 41 (1981), pp. 18-25, 34.
       Survey of career and interests. (JS)

RICHARD COWPER

F65   Elliot, Jeffrey. "Interview: Richard Cowper." FN,
       No. 36 (1981), pp. 17-24, 30.
          A full account of Cowper's background, including
       a childhood meeting with H. G. Wells. Comments on
       own writing. (JS)

F. MARION CRAWFORD

F66   Moran, John C. _An F. Marion Crawford Companion_.
       Westport, CT and London: Greenwood Press, 1981.
           This handbook begins with a critical introduction
       by Edward Wagenknecht, and includes an essay on
       Crawford's romanticism by Donald Sidney-Fryer and a
       tribute to Crawford from Russell Kirk. Moran's own
       long introduction outlines Crawford's life and work.
       Then, biographical and literary chronologies are
       provided, listing every known event and work in
       Crawford's career. Other features include biograph-
       ical sketches of Crawford's friends and associates,
       an alphabetical listing of every place-name which
       appears in Crawford's forty-odd novels, a listing of
       all the characters in Crawford's works, and an
       indexed selection of representative passages from
       Crawford's books. A complete bibliographical his-
       tory of Crawford's writing rounds out this defini-
       tive literary reference. (MBT)

RAY CUMMINGS

F67   Ladd, Thyrill. "Ray Cummings: A Meeting." Introd.
       The Girl in the Golden Atom. By Ray Cummings.
       Westport, CT: Hyperion Press, 1974.
           An account of Ladd's friendship with Cummings
       which reveals previously unpublished details of
       Cummings' biography. (AT)

L. SPRAGUE DE CAMP   (See also C26, F137)

F68   de Camp, Catherine Crook (See F69)

F69   de Camp, L. Sprague, and Catherine Crook de Camp.
       Footprints on Sand: A Literary Sampler. Chicago:
       Advent, 1981.
           A selection of stories, verse, nonfiction, and
       excerpts from almost every facet of the de Camps'
       diverse writings. Included is a section of tributes
       from such friends and associates as Robert Heinlein,
       Lin Carter, Isaac Asimov, Poul Anderson, Andrew
       Offutt, Patricia Jackson, and George Scithers.
       (MBT)

LESTER DEL REY (See also D11, F212)

F70   Schweitzer, Darrell. "Lester del Rey." In _Science
       Fiction Voices #5_. Ed. Darrell Schweitzer. San
       Bernardino, CA: Borgo Press, 1981, pp. 26-35.
           Del Rey focuses on critics and criticism, de-
       scribing the role of the critic, the nature of
       criticism, the value of the critic, and the status
       of science fiction criticism. Talks about a number
       of other subjects, including aspects of his life and
       work. (JME)

SAMUEL R. DELANY (See also B20, C08, C09, C34, D03,
D24, F213, F248)

F71   Eastman, Donald R. "The Strategies of Survival:
       Cybernetic Differences in The Einstein Inter-
       section." Extrapolation, 22 (1981), 270-76.
           Crux of novel is the importance of change, an
       effort to grasp difference that by its nature is
       beyond language. (JS)

F72   Gawron, Jean Mark, introd. Triton. By Samuel R.
       Delany. Boston: Gregg Press, 1977.
           "Triton, a novel of many worlds and a number of
       logics, may be read as an exploration of a par-
       ticular logical space (Brain Helstrom's) and the
       particular world it pervades (Triton)." (AT)

F73   Hartwell, David G., introd. Empire Star. By Samuel
       R. Delany. Boston: Gregg Press, 1977.
           Analyzes the novel as a halfway point between
       Alfred Bester's The Stars My Destination and
       Delany's own later novel, Dahlgren. (AT)

F74   Milicia, Joseph, introd. The Fall of the Towers.
       By Samuel R. Delany. Boston: Gregg Press, 1977.
           Discusses the structural patterns that unify the
       novels in this trilogy and Delany's use of the sense
       of randomness as an aspect of both the plot and the
       theme. (AT)

       AUGUST DERLETH

F75   Moskowitz, Sam. "I Remember Derleth." Starship,
       No. 41 (1981), pp. 7-14.
           Describes a visit to Derleth's home by Moskowitz,
       along with many other encounters with Derleth.
       While not an intimate acquaintance, Moskowitz was in
       a good position to observe Derleth over the years
       and to offer comments on business practices, life
       style, and personality. (JS)

       PHILIP K. DICK (See also B05)

F76   Bertrand, Frank C. "Encounters with Reality: P. K.
       Dick's A Scanner Darkly." PS, 1 (March 1981),
       12-15.
           Ponders Dick's juggling of realities as perceived
       by the two role-personalities of the same character,
       compared to the philosophy of Pierre Teilhard de
       Chardin. (JS)

F77   -------. "Kant's 'Noumenal Self' and Doppelganger
       in P. K. Dick's A Scanner Darkly." PS, 1 (Summer
       1981), 69-80.
           Discusses in Kant's terms the confusion of char-
       acters, "schizomania," in Arctor/Fred, finding Fred
       the noumenal/non-temporal self and Arctor the
       phenomenal/empirical self--leaving unanswered the
       novel's question: Which is the real one? (JS)

F78   Brown, Steve. "The Two Tractates of Philip K.
       Dick." SFR, No. 38 (1981), pp. 11-12.

Examines the paradox of commercial acclaim and
artistic invention, arguing that, in the case of
Dick, the latter has found a place in "the museum to
display his chunk of wood." (JME)

F79   Goodlife, Fax, introd. Vulcan's Hammer. By Philip
       K. Dick. Boston: Gregg Press, 1979.
       Though written in 1960, Vulcan's Hammer articu-
       lates the current fear that the computer will rule
       the world. (AT)

F80   Hartwell, David G., introd. Counter-Clock World.
       By Philip K. Dick. Boston: Gregg Press, 1979.
       Argues "that Counter-Clock World is an imperfect
       novel of science fiction but a serious work of
       considerable depth and richness, a complex meta-
       physical novel with vivid characters in an absurd
       environment." (AT)

F81   Levack, Daniel J. H. PKD: A Philip K. Dick Biblio-
       graphy. San Francisco: Underwood-Miller, 1981.
       The first of a projected series of matched-format
       annotated pictorial bibliographies by Daniel Levack.
       All points and states of Dick's first editions are
       clearly described, with 148 annotations, 198 repro-
       ductions, and 950 descriptive citations. Both
       foreign and English-language publications are in-
       cluded. All of Dick's published works through
       mid-1981 are listed. Also issued in paperback.
       (MBT)

F82   Miesel, Sandra, introd. Eye in the Sky. By Philip
       K. Dick. Boston: Gregg Press, 1979.
       The novel established Dick's literary formulas:
       his "method of using imaginary universes to drama-
       tize the subjective nature of reality"; the fears
       about schizophrenia; his references to popular
       culture; the fear of extremes and the corollary
       "fear of all systems because they are
       institutionalized extremism." (AT)

F83   Platt, Charles, introd. The Zap Gun. By Philip K.
       Dick. Boston: Gregg Press, 1979.
       Compares The Zap Gun to Vonnegut's Slaughter-
       house-Five and calls it a celebration of the
       vagaries of the human condition. (AT)

F84   Silverberg, Robert, introd. Clans of the Alphane
       Moon. By Philip K. Dick. Boston: Gregg Press,
       1979.
       Argues that the novel is a minor work built
       around the theme that there is very little to be
       trusted. (AT)

F85   Stathis, Louis, introd. Time Out of Joint. By
       Philip K. Dick. Boston: Gregg Press, 1979.
       Demonstrates that the novel "blends the pacing,
       textural fiber and characterizational detail of the

mainstream with the imagination and consistency of
visions of science fiction." Also calls this work a
transitional book between Dick's early Ace novels
and his later masterpieces, The Man in the High
Castle, The Three Stigmata of Palmer Eldritch, and
Ubik. (AT)

F86   Thurston, Robert, introd. The Game-Players of
       Titan. By Philip K. Dick. Boston: Gregg Press,
       1979.
           Argues that Dick's characters' loss of control
       often leads them to a better perception of reality.
       (AT)

CHARLES DICKENS

F87   Bailey, K. V. "Spaceships, Little Nell and the
       Sinister Cardboard Man: A Study of Dickens as
       Fantasist and as a Precursor of SF." Foundation,
       No. 21 (1981), pp. 34-47.
           Focusing on images of arks, mechanical figures,
       and railways, Bailey suggests that science fiction
       may owe something more specific to Dickens than the
       general debt that all twentieth-century literature
       owes to him. (DMH)

THOMAS M. DISCH (See also I04)

F88   Hartwell, David G., introd. The Genocides. By
       Thomas M. Disch. Boston: Gregg Press, 1978.
           Critical reaction to The Genocides and suppos-
       itions about the reasons for Disch's unpopularity
       with many American readers. (AT)

F89   Thurston, Robert, introd. The Early Science Fiction
       Stories of Thomas M. Disch. By Thomas M. Disch.
       Boston: Gregg Press, 1977.
           Argues that Disch's fiction confronts reality
       with romance, humor with seriousness, wit with
       slapstick, and beauty with grotesquerie. (AT)

STEPHEN R. DONALDSON

F90   Wilson, Andrew J. "Melding for Beginners: Language
       and Names in 'The Illearth War.'" Dark Horizons,
       No. 24 (1981), pp. 9-13.
           An exploration into the diversity and conse-
       quences of nomenclature in Donaldson's novel in his
       "Chronicles of Thomas Covenant" series. His obses-
       sion with words is a source of weakness but does not
       undermine the effectiveness of his work. (JF)

WILLIAM S. DOXEY

F91   Doxey, William S. "The Star Poem: The Creation of
       an SF Epic." Portland Review, 27, No. 2 (1981),
       56-57.
           The author discusses his approach to the creation

of an epic science fiction poem of 555 five-line
stanzas, using as a plot and characters much that is
traditional in science fiction prose. A summary and
extracts of the work are provided. (TWH)

ARTHUR CONAN DOYLE

F92   Batory, Dana Martin. "The Real Professor Challen-
         ger." Megavore, No. 13 (1981), pp. 42-47.
         The hero of Sir Arthur Conan Doyle's science
fiction novels, Professor George Edward Challenger,
is modeled directly after Doyle's old friend, Dr.
George Budd. (MBT)

GARDNER DOZOIS (See B11)

LORD DUNSANY

F93   Cantrell, Brent. "British Fairy Tradition in The
         King of Elfland's Daughter." The Romantist, No. 4-5
         (1980-81), pp. 51-53.
         The fairy elements in Dunsany's 1924 novel are
examined in terms of their actual folklore content.
(SE)

F94   Schweitzer, Darrell. "The Novels of Lord Dunsany:
         Part 2." Mythlore, No. 26 (1981), pp. 39-41.
         Discussion/critiques of Dunsany's last novels--
according to Schweitzer, rather tired and unsuc-
cessful works. (JS)

LAWRENCE DURRELL

F95   Mablekos, Carole. "Lawrence Durrell's Tunc and
         Nunquam: Rebirth Now or Never." The Sphinx, No. 13
         (1981), pp. 48-54.
         Durrell's two-volume science fiction work aban-
dons the concern with the nuances of psyche he
displayed in The Alexandria Quartet and concentrates
instead upon theme, criticizing society's tendency
"to reduce everything to a commodity." (TPD)

E. R. EDDISON (See B28)

SUZETTE HADIN ELGIN (See I05)

HARLAN ELLISON (See also C26, I06)

F96   Ellison, Harlan. "Memoir: I Have No Mouth, and I
         Must Scream." In Fantastic Lives. Ed. Martin H.
         Greenberg. Carbondale: Southern Illinois Univ.
         Press, 1981, pp. 1-19.
         Ellison comments on the writing of his famous
story and on the supererogatory nature of science
fiction scholarship. Bibliography of his major
works follows. (TPD)

F97   Staicar, Tom. "Harlan Ellison on the Art of Making
         Waves." TZM, No. 8 (1981), pp. 15-25.

A characteristically outspoken interview in which
Ellison voices his disdain for genre labels applied
to himself, discusses self-promotion tactics, avows
the honest intent behind his work, and vents his
spleen at publishers who shortchange writers. (SE)

GEORGE ALLAN ENGLAND

F98   England, George Allan. "The Fantastic in Fiction."
       Introd. Darkness and Dawn. By George Allan Eng-
       land. Westport, CT: Hyperion Press, 1974.
       Author's commentary on many of his stories on
       pseudoscientific themes published between 1906-1923.
       (AT)

EVANGELINE WALTON ENSLEY (See E28)

DENNIS ETCHISON

F99   Schweitzer, Darrell. "Interview: Dennis Etchison."
       FN, No. 34 (1981), pp. 16-19, 30.
       A discussion of career, influences, going much
       more deeply than many interviews into motivations
       and procedures of being a horror writer. (JS)

PHILIP JOSE FARMER (See also F49, F211, F267)

F100   Farmer, Philip Jose. "Maps and Spasms." In
       Fantastic Lives. Ed. Martin H. Greenberg.
       Carbondale: Southern Illinois Univ. Press, 1981, pp.
       20-56.
       Farmer discusses his life in science fiction to
       1952 with detailed attention given to his beginnings
       as a science fiction writer. Bibliography of his
       major science fiction works follows. (TPD)

CHARLES G. FINNEY (See C26)

ROBERT L. FORWARD

F101   Krasnoff, Barbara. "Interview: Robert L. Forward."
       Future Life, No. 28 (1981), pp. 33-35.
       The author of Dragon's Egg explains his scien-
       tific view of things. (MBT)

RAYMOND Z. GALLUN (See also I07)

F102   Elliot, Jeffrey M. "Interview: Raymond Z. Gallun."
       Thrust, No. 17 (1981), pp. 6-13.
       This retrospective interview focuses on Gallun's
       life and work, reviewing his fifty-year career in
       the science fiction field, as well as many of his
       120-odd published stories and books. (JME)

ALAN GARNER (See also C31)

F103   Philip, Neil. A Fine Anger: A Critical Introduction
       to the Work of Alan Garner. New York: Philomel,
       1981.

Traces Garner's development from his straight-
forward magic fantasy, The Weirdstone of Brisingham
(1960) to the highly acclaimed Stone Book quartet
(1976). Primary and secondary bibliographies.
(MBT)

MARK S. GETSON

F104   Monteleone, Thomas F., introd. Lords of the Starship. By Mark S. Getson. Boston: Gregg Press,
1978.
Argues that Lords of the Starship, despite its
weak characterizations and murky plot, succeeds as
myth, allegory, and future history. (AT)

TOM GODWIN (See C14)

WILLIAM GOLDING

F105   Walker, Jeanne Murray. "Reciprocity and Exchange in
William Golding's The Inheritors." SFS, 8 (1981),
297-310.
Though this second of Golding's novels has been
neglected, it makes brilliant sense as science
fiction and should not be misclassified as a parable
or moral fable; the novel projects a social system
more tenable than the two it contrasts, thus ef-
fecting the reader like extrapolative science
fiction. (DMH)

PHYLLIS GOTLIEB

F106   Lynn, Elizabeth A., introd. Sunburst. By Phyllis
Gotlieb. Boston: Gregg Press, 1978.
Traces the use, in science fiction, of the relationship between a normal society and its super-
normal children, analyzes Sunburst, and compares it
favorably to other novels about superchildren. (AT)

RON GOULART

F107   Shapiro, David, introd. After Things Fell Apart.
By Ron Goulart. Boston: Gregg Press, 1977.
In this novel Goulart attempts to revitalize, pay
homage to, and lampoon conventional detective
stories through a parody set in the future. (AT)

CHARLES L. GRANT (See F132)

PERCY GREG

F108   Moskowitz, Sam. "Across the Zodiac: A Major Turning
Point in Science Fiction." Introd. Across the
Zodiac. By Percy Greg. Westport, CT: Hyperion
Press, 1974.
Describes Across the Zodiac as an early dystopia
and the first novel to scientifically describe a
journey farther from the Earth than the Moon. (AT)

GEORGE GRIFFITH

F109   Moskowitz, Sam. "George Griffith: Forgotten 'Hawk'
       of Science Fiction." Introd. The Angel of the
       Revolution. By George Griffith. Westport, CT:
       Hyperion Press, 1974.
          Brief biography of Griffith, an important future
       war author, a contemporary of H. G. Wells who in-
       fluenced an entire generation of British science
       fiction authors. (AT)

F110   -------. "George Griffith, Influential Popular-
       izer." Introd. Olga Romanoff. By George Griffith.
       Westport, CT: Hyperion Press, 1974.
          Relates the publishing history of Olga Romanoff
       and demonstrates Griffith's influence on H. G. Wells
       and George du Maurier. (AT)

JAMES GUNN (See F116)

H. RIDER HAGGARD

F111   Katz, Wendy R. "Rider Haggard and the Empire of the
       Imagination." English Literature in Transition
       (1880-1920), 23 (1980), 115-24.
          Accounts for the attraction of Haggard's adven-
       ture fiction (especially the Ayesha novels) as
       propaganda of the Empire, concealing the "greed of
       imperialism" but preserving the fiction's popular
       emotional appeal. (JAG)

J. B. S. HALDANE (See C18, E20)

JOE HALDEMAN

F112   Gordon, Joan Lois. "Inside Science Fiction and the
       Fiction of Joe Haldeman." Ph.D. dissertation, Uni-
       versity Of Iowa, 1981; DAI, 42: 3156A.
          Through examples of Haldeman's works, this dis-
       sertation examines the way in which science fiction
       is joined to the mainstream of literary traditions.
       (PA)

EDMOND HAMILTON (See E23, E25)

CHARLES L. HARNESS (See also B05)

F113   Vernon, William D. "Charles L. Harness, the Paradox
       Man." SFC, No. 14 (1981), pp. 25-28.
          A survey and commentary on Harness' science
       fiction works. (MBT)

M. JOHN HARRISON

F114   Fowler, Christopher. "The Last Rebel: An Interview
       with M. John Harrison." Foundation, No. 23 (1981),
       pp. 5-30.

A two-part interview (from January 1977 and
December 1980) with a writer who has been neglected
somewhat by the science fiction establishment since
he refuses to pigeon-hole his own work. Harrison
discusses, in part, this "isolation" of his career
to date. (DMH)

MILO HASTINGS

F115 Moskowitz, Sam. "Milo Hastings: Prophet of Totali-
      tarianism." Introd. City of Endless Night. By
      Milo Hastings. Westport, CT: Hyperion Press, 1974.
         This early anti-Utopian novel, reflecting the
      experiences of World War I and anticipating Nazi
      doctrine, was also the finest achievement of the
      Physical Culture school of science fiction, led by
      "Bernard McFadden's attempts to teach proper living
      and realistic standards of morality through fic-
      tion." (AT)

NATHANIEL HAWTHORNE (See E16, E19, F176)

ROBERT HEINLEIN (See also D19, F09)

F116 Gunn, James. "The Grand Master--Robert A.
      Heinlein." Starship, No. 41 (1981), pp. 31-34.
         Actually the introduction to the Gregg Press
      edition of The Puppet Masters. A survey of Hein-
      lein's development, increased control of longer
      stories, centering on The Puppet Masters. Relates
      that novel to the rest of Heinlein's work in themes:
      freedom based on acceptance of responsibility, duty
      to grow wise and educate others, importance of
      competence (understanding of process). Discusses
      the style in what Gunn considers Heinlein's most
      artistically successful novel. (JS)

F117 Hartwell, David G., introd. Destination Moon. By
      Robert A. Heinlein. Boston: Gregg Press, 1979.
         History of Heinlein's efforts to film the first
      Hollywood movie about a trip to the moon; a com-
      parison of the film to the novella of the same
      title; and an excerpt, reprinted from Future Tense,
      of John Brosnan's discussion of Heinlein's other
      science fiction film, Project Moonbase. (AT)

F118 -------, introd. The Door into Summer. By Robert
      A. Heinlein. Boston: Gregg Press, 1979.
         The Door into Summer demonstrates Heinlein's use
      of science fiction techniques borrowed from H. G.
      Wells. (AT)

FRANK HERBERT (See also E01, E02, E13)

F119 Curtis, Keith (See F120)

F120 Dowling, Terry, Keith Curtis, and Joseph Nicholas.
      "Interview with Frank Herbert." Science Fiction, 3
      (1981), 96-108.

A lengthy interview conducted with Herbert over a
two-day period in June 1981 at Advention in
Adelaide, Australia. (DMH)

F121 Nicholas, Joseph (See F120)

F122 O'Reilly, Timothy. Frank Herbert. Recognitions
series. New York. Frederick Ungar, 1981.
    This first book-length study of Herbert provides
commentary on fifteen novels and numerous stories,
essays, letters, and poetry. It is enriched by a
series of interviews with Herbert. Primary and
secondary bibliographies. Also issued in paperback.
(MBT)

F123 Tait, Steven. "The Implication of 'Battle Language'
in the Dune Universe." P*S*F*Q, No. 6 (1981), p.
15.
    Argues that Herbert's phrase, "battle language,"
is not only a unifying point for much of what is
stated explicitly in Dune, but is also an implied
statement about that society. (JME)

WILLIAM HOPE HODGSON (See also C12)

F124 Ashley, Mike. "The Fiction of William Hope Hodgson:
A Working Bibliography." SFC, No. 15 (1981), pp.
15-18.
    A listing of Hodgson's books and short stories
published in English. (MBT)

JAMES HOGAN (See D04)

ALDOUS HUXLEY

F125 Aldridge, Alexandra. "Brave New World and the
Mechanist/Vitalist Controversy." Comparative
Literature Studies, 17 (1980), 116-32.
    Claims that Huxley was influenced by Alfred North
Whitehead and other antimechanists, imagining in
Brave New World a dystopia created by mechanistic
science. (JAG)

F126 Bass, Eben E. Aldous Huxley: An Annotated Bibliography of Criticism. New York and London: Garland,
1981.
    Includes information on articles and books about
Huxley, reviews of his work, and dissertations; all
English-language criticism is annotated. Provides a
broad view of the range in critical attitudes toward
Huxley, from the beginning of his career in 1916 to
the present. (MBT)

F127 Larsen, Peter M. "Synthetic Myths in Aldous
Huxley's Brave New World: A Note." English Studies,
62 (1981), 506-08.
    Synthetic myths, powerful ideological tools which
mask opposition and conflict within a society,

pervade the society of Brave New World. The myths
are cast in five forms: jingles, nursery rhymes, new
and rewritten proverbs and pseudostatements; and all
are designed for mindless parroting. (JAG)

DAVID IRELAND

F128   Hay, Sheridan. "An Interview with David Ireland."
Science Fiction, 3 (1981), 109-16.
   An interview with this Australian novelist which
emphasizes his prewriting techniques of keeping
extensive notebooks. (DMH)

M. R. JAMES

F129   Ashley, Mike. "M. R. James." TZM (December 1981),
pp. 55-59.
   Bio-critical survey of the ghost story master,
with discussion of those directly influenced by him.
(SE)

DAVID H. KELLER

F130   Ashley, Mike. "David H. Keller Bibliography: Part
I." Fantasy Macabre, No. 2 (April 1981), pp. 23-37.
   Keller's fiction exhaustively listed: books and
pamphlets, magazine serials and short fiction. All
known appearances are listed. (SE)

F131   Moskowitz, Sam, introd. Life Everlasting and Other
Tales of Science, Fantasy, and Horror. By David H.
Keller. Ed. Sam Moskowitz. Westport, CT: Hyperion
Press, 1974.
   A brief biography of Keller which demonstrates
the influences of his childhood and his career as a
psychiatrist on his writing. (AT)

STEPHEN KING (See also B17, H13)

F132   Grant, Charles L. "Stephen King: 'I Like to go for
the Jugular.'" TZM (April 1981), pp. 18-23.
   Interview with the best-selling horror fiction
writer in which King discusses his influences and
his opinions of the horror genre. (SE)

F133   Stewart, Robert. "Filmedia: The Rest of King."
Starship, No. 41 (1981), pp. 45-46.
   Interview in which King discusses his early
writing career and comments on a few other contem-
porary writers such as Fritz Leiber and J. Ramsey
Campbell. (JS)

DAMON KNIGHT (See I03)

DEAN R. KOONTZ (See I09)

C. M. KORNBLUTH (See also E09)

F134   West, D. "The Right Sort of People." _Foundation_,
        No. 21 (1981), pp. 17-26.
           A concerted attack on Kornbluth's story, "The
        Marching Morons," in which West argues that the
        images for reason and logic actually conceal deep
        fantasies of revenge and power. (DMH)

        R. A. LAFFERTY

F135   Lafferty, R. A. "The Case of the Moth-eaten Magi-
        cian." In _Fantastic Lives_. Ed. Martin H. Green-
        berg. Carbondale: Southern Illinois Univ. Press,
        1981, pp. 57-78.
           Lafferty comments on early pulp science fiction
        and compares it, unfavorably, to his own more "mag-
        ical" kind. He points out that the early pulps
        always disappointed because they never delivered
        what the covers promised. Bibliography of his major
        science fiction works follows. (TPD)

F136   Platt, Charles, introd. _The Devil Is Dead_. By R.
        A. Lafferty. Boston: Gregg Press, 1977.
           Explains that since Lafferty's work mixes classic
        American tall tale methods with more conventional
        mythic archetypes and elements of conventional
        science fiction and fantasy, his difficulty in
        getting his work published is due to the catego-
        rization of science fiction. (AT)

        HAROLD LAMB

F137   de Camp, L. Sprague, introd. _Marching Sands_. By
        Harold Lamb. Westport, CT: Hyperion Press, 1974.
           Brief biography of Lamb, whose tales of histor-
        ical adventure influenced Robert E. Howard and whose
        favorite theme was East-versus-West. (AT)

        J. SHERIDAN LE FANU

F138   Sutton, David. "The Invisible Prince." _Dark
        Horizons_, No. 23 (1981), pp. 8-13.
           An examination of the life and work of Le Fanu.
        His best stories are discussed and comparisons made
        with H. P. Lovecraft and M. R. James. (JF)

F139   Veeder, William. "_Carmilla_: The Arts of Repres-
        sion." _Texas Studies in Literature and Language_, 22
        (1980), 197-223.
           In a penetrating psychological analysis of
        Carmilla, Veeder asserts that Le Fanu's female
        protagonists, Laura and Carmilla, are both victims
        of the dual desires of the vampire, human and lesbi-
        an, and this duality is the result of the repressed
        desires of women in Victorian society. (TPD)

URSULA K. LE GUIN (See also B20, C13, C14, C34, D03, D14, I10)

F140   Barr, Marleen S. "Charles Bronson, Samurai, and
       Other Feminine Images: A Transactional Response to
       The Left Hand of Darkness." In Future Females. Ed.
       Marleen S. Barr. Bowling Green, OH: Bowling Green
       State Univ. Popular Press, 1981, pp. 138-54.
          When Barr examines her responses to the mediation
       of communal and nationalistic values in The Left
       Hand of Darkness, she finds in herself "a refusal to
       exchange my individualistic career goals for my
       society's prevailing antifeminist notions." (TPD)

F141   Bucknall, Barbara J. Ursula K. Le Guin. Recogni-
       tions series. New York: Frederick Ungar, 1981.
          The first single-authored book-length study of
       one of the most important writers to emerge in the
       1960s. Follows Le Guin's growth from the early
       Hainish novels, through her Earthsea children's
       fantasy series, to the "social" science fiction of
       The Left Hand of Darkness, The Lathe of Heaven, and
       The Dispossessed. Includes discussion of Le Guin's
       short stories. Secondary bibliography. Also issued
       in paperback. (MBT)

F142   Holland, Norman N. "You, U. K. Le Guin." In Future
       Females. Ed. Marleen S. Barr. Bowling Green OH:
       Bowling Green State Univ. Popular Press, 1981, pp.
       125-37.
          A reader-response critique seeking the central
       meaning of The Left Hand of Darkness by means of an
       evocative fusion of commentary, meditation, free
       association, and intense personal rhapsody. (TPD)

F143   LaBar, Martin. "Slipping the Truth in Edgewise."
       Christianity Today, 25 (March 1981), 38-39.
          A Christian writer examines the work of Le Guin
       and the Taoist philosophy that pervades much of her
       fiction. (PA)

F144   Lake, David J. "Le Guin's Twofold Vision: Contrary
       Image Sets in The Left Hand of Darkness." SFS, 8
       (1981), 156-64.
          The richness of the novel allows for the detec-
       tion of numerous pairs of images that Lake groups
       into what he calls the "cold team" and the "warm
       team" and then discusses in the context of Blake's
       "Contraries." He concludes that Le Guin has less
       sense of progress than Blake. (DMH)

F145   Widmer, Kingsley. "Utopian, Dystopian, Diatopian
       Libertarianism: Le Guin's The Dispossessed." The
       Sphinx, No. 13 (1981), pp. 55-66.
          In contrast to the "callowly optimistic social
       engineering" of Bellamy's Looking Backward and
       Skinner's Walden Two, Le Guin's utopian society
       engages in endless friction and change in a dia

lectical mode which Widmer suggests we call "diatopian." (TPD)

TANITH LEE

F146   Schweitzer, Darrell. "Interview: Tanith Lee." FN,
No. 42 (1981), pp. 12-15.
Discusses, playfully but with underlying seri-
ousness, Lee's attraction to the supernatural and
how it affects her writing. (JS)

FRITZ LEIBER (See also D19, I06)

F147   Leiber, Fritz, introd. Swords and Deviltry. By
Fritz Leiber. Boston: Gregg Press, 1977.
Author's reminiscence of his creation, with Harry
Fischer, of Fafhrd and the Gray Mouser. (AT)

F148   Leiber, Justin. "Science Fiction Worlds." PS, 1
(1981), 52-60.
Includes material from introduction to Gregg
Press edition of The Worlds of Fritz Leiber. Tries
to distinguish science fiction from mere retelling
of action-adventure tales and to determine what
makes good science fiction. Centers on stories in
The Worlds of Fritz Leiber, listing different aspects of created worlds that make the stories
rewarding. (JS)

F149   Silbersack, John, introd. The Change War. By Fritz
Leiber. Boston: Gregg Press, 1978.
The Change War stories "reflect Leiber's fascina-
tion with the instability of much of modern American
life" and "test the boundaries of science fiction
and gothic horror as they apply to modern life."
(AT)

F150   Thurston, Robert, introd. The Big Time. By Fritz
Leiber. Boston: Gregg Press, 1976.
Concludes that the best features of Leiber's work
derive from his interest in the theater. (AT)

JUSTIN LEIBER   (See D19, F148)

STANISLAW LEM (See also C15)

F151   Michaelson, L. W. "A Conversation with Stanislaw
Lem." Amazing (January 1981), pp. 116-19.
An interview in which Lem mentions he needs and
wants no more money, and opinions on American politics, the Polish church, and comparisons of his
fiction with that of American writers. (TWH)

MADELEINE L'ENGLE (See C31)

DORIS LESSING

F152   Bailey, Chris. "So, Who Needs Characters Anyway?"
Vector, No. 105 (1981), pp. 19-21.

An examination of Lessing's <u>Shikasta</u> with particular emphasis on the role of the protagonist and its
theme of destroyed human potential. (JF)

F153 Cleary, Rochelle Diane. "A Study of Marriage in
      Doris Lessing's Fiction.: Ph.D. dissertation, State
      University of New York at Stony Brook, 1981; <u>DAI</u>,
      42: 4831A.
         Lessing's writings in her mainstream and science
      fiction have often centered on marriage as a theme,
      reflecting her most important ideas about the indi-
      vidual and society. One of the works examined here
      is <u>The Marriages Between Zones Three, Four and Five</u>.
      (PA)

F154 Gomoll, Jeanne. "Doris Lessing: Canopus in Argos."
      <u>P*S*F*Q</u>, No. 6 (1981), pp. 14, 17.
         Gomoll reviews Lessing's two most recent novels,
      <u>Shikasta</u> and <u>Marriages</u>, the first two of a five-
      volume series of books chronicling the epic history
      and geography of Earth, as seen by a far superior
      and distant civilization. (JME)

F155 Sawyer, Andy. "An Interim Report from the Archives:
      The SF of Doris Lessing." <u>Vector</u>, No. 103 (1981),
      pp. 5-12.
         Doris Lessing was regarded as a writer of main-
      stream fiction who occasionally employed science
      fictional concepts, but she has now fully entered
      the genre with her <u>Canopus in Argo</u> series. (JF)

F156 Seligman, Dee. <u>Doris Lessing: An Annotated Bibli-
      ography of Criticism</u>. Westport, CT and London:
      Greenwood Press, 1981.
         A comprehensive listing of works on Lessing
      through 1978. [Not seen.] (MBT)

      C. S. LEWIS (See also C31, D21, E01, E03-07, E11,
      E15, E21)

F157 Becker, Joan Quall. "Patterns of Guilt and Grace in
      the Development and Function of Character in C. S.
      Lewis' Romances." Ph.D. dissertation, University of
      Washington, 1981; <u>DAI</u>, 42: 2361A.
         A study of the achievements and failures of Lewis
      in the development and use of characterization in
      his imaginative fiction. Focus is on the protago-
      nists of <u>The Chronicles of Narnia</u>. (PA)

F158 Christensen, Michael. "On Lizards and Stallions."
      <u>CSL</u>, 12 (February 1981), 1-5.
         A critical reading of <u>The Great Divorce</u>, demon-
      strating that the work has two levels of meaning.
      While Lewis' work may be read on the simpler level
      of allegory, it has deeper meaning at the level of
      myth fantasy. (JAG)

F159 Fitzpatrick, John. "Lewis and Wagner." <u>CSL</u>, 12
      (October 1981), 1-9.

Traces the influences of Wagner's operas, especially those of the ring cycle, through several of
Lewis' works. (JAG)

F160   Glover, Donald E. C. S. Lewis: The Art of Enchant-
ment. Athens: Ohio Univ. Press, 1981.
Following an introductory section examining
Lewis' critical theory, this study contains full
discussions of sixteen works, including a chapter on
Lewis' letters. Also issued in paperback. (MBT)

F161   Hannay, Margaret Patterson. C. S. Lewis. New York:
Frederick Ungar, 1981.
In a style unhampered by academic jargon, Hannay
offers a biographical sketch, concise summaries of
each major work, a survey of Lewis' major themes,
and an analysis of his allusive and compelling
style. (MBT)

F162   Lindvall, Terrence Roy. "C. S. Lewis' Theory of
Communication." Ph.D. dissertation, University of
Southern California, 1981; DAI, 42: 19A.
An examination of Lewis' work uncovered his
theory of communication, stressing nonmanipulation,
reason, and ethics. Lewis enacted this principle in
all his writings, including his well-known imaginative fiction. (PA)

F163   Patterson, Nancy-Lou. "Banquet at Belbury: Festival
and Horror in That Hideous Strength." Mythlore, No.
29 (1981), pp. 7-14, 42.
Some readers are put off by the massacre at
N.I.C.E. headquarters that forms the climax of
Lewis' novel. In detailed examination of the pas-
sage, Patterson justifies the brutality as
animals'/nature's response to violations by devil-
inspired scientists, paralleling actions in other
Romance tales. (JS)

F164   -------. "The Host of Heaven: Astrological and
Other Images of Divinity in the Fantasies of C. S.
Lewis (Part II)." Mythlore, No. 26 (1981), pp.
13-21.
An examination of the Narnia series and Till We
Have Faces, chiefly explicating Lewis' use of a
variety of myths in predominantly Christian fantasy.
(JS)

F165   Price, Steven. "Freedom and Nature in Perelandra."
Mythlore, No. 29 (1981), pp. 38-40, 42.
A discussion of the novel in light of Lewis'
"belief that true humanity is achieved only by
spontaneous, free-will choices coupled with an
acceptance of change as the essential nature of life
and reality." (JS)

F166   Rogers, Katherin A. "The Mirror of the Divine:
Christian Platonism in C. S. Lewis." PS, 1 (1981),
18-25.

Explains how Lewis shows the world as a reflec-
tion of God, stressing necessity for humans to
penetrate shadow and find reality. (JS)

F167   Smith, Robert Houston. <u>Patches of Godlight: The
Pattern of Thought of C. S. Lewis</u>. Athens: University of Georgia Press, 1981.
A description of Lewis' philosophy of religion in
which Smith attempts to show that Lewis had a rich,
integrated philosophical frame of reference that
undergirded--and occasionally deviated from--his
Christian beliefs. (MBT)

F168   Watson, James Darrell. "A Reader's Guide to C. S.
Lewis: His Fiction." Ph.D. dissertation, East Texas
State University, 1981; <u>DAI</u>, 42: 2692A.
A study of the primary theme of Lewis' fiction,
the salvation from supernatural evil. (PA)

DAVID LINDSAY

F169   Pohl, Joy. "Dualities in David Lindsay's <u>A Voyage
to Arcturus</u>." <u>Extrapolation</u>, 22 (1981), 164-70.
Describes splits in characterization and setting.
(JS)

F170   Raff, Melvin. "The Structure of <u>A Voyage to
Arcturus</u>." <u>Studies in Scottish Literature</u>, 15
(1980), 262-68.
Demonstrates that the novel contains an intricate
pattern of tripartite divisions. Contends that the
frame of the novel is Lindsay's examination of the
relationships between feeling, the character's
relation to the world, and existence. (JAG)

F171   Sellin, Bernard. <u>The Life and Work of David
Lindsay</u>. Trans. Kenneth Gunnell. New York and
London: Cambridge Univ. Press, 1981.
As a result of renewed interest in Lindsay,
Sellin has written the first comprehensive study of
the author's life and work, in which he analyzes the
thematic patterns of his settings, plots, and char-
acters. (MBT)

JACK LONDON

F172   Seed, D. "The Apocalyptic Structure of Jack
London's <u>The Iron Heel</u>." <u>Jack London Newsletter</u>, 13
(1980), 1-11.
Analyzes London's use of apocalypse to point to a
social decadence which increases as the novel pro-
gresses, the historical process of the socialist
movement culminating in the revolution against the
repressive Iron Heel in the chaos of mob violence in
Chicago. (JAG)

FRANK BELKNAP LONG

F173   Schweitzer, Darrell. "Frank Belknap Long." In
       Science Fiction Voices #5. Ed. Darrell Schweitzer.
       San Bernardino, CA: Borgo Press, 1981, pp. 41-48.
       Long reviews his rich and varied career, with
       specific emphasis on his personal and professional
       relationship with H. P. Lovecraft. (JME)

BARRY LONGYEAR

F174   Klein, Jay Jay. "Biolog." Analog (April 1981), p.
       85.
       A biography of the relatively new writer Barry
       Longyear, mentioning his early stories and awards,
       as well as his writing techniques. (TWH)

HOWARD PHILLIPS LOVECRAFT (See also C16, D21, E17,
E19, F173)

F175   Bell, Joseph. Howard Phillips Lovecraft: The Books
       1915-1981. Toronto: Soft Books, 1981 pbk.
       A bibliography of Lovecraft's books, collabora-
       tions, essays, fiction, revisions, and verse. (MBT)

F176   Burleson, Donald R. "H. P. Lovecraft: The Hawthorne
       Influence." Extrapolation, 22 (1981), 262-69.
       Hawthorne influenced Lovecraft in his setting of
       stories in New England, fusion of personality with
       place, psychopomp (catcher of departing souls),
       power of past myths in present. (JS)

F177   -------. "The Mythic Hero Archetype in 'The Dunwich
       Horror.'" Lovecraft Studies, 1 (Spring 1981), 3-9.
       The eight stages of the mythic hero (or "mono-
       myth") are discerned in Lovecraft's major novelette.
       (SE)

F178   Joshi, S. T. H. P. Lovecraft and Lovecraft Criti-
       cism: An Annotated Bibliography. Serif series, No.
       38. Kent, OH: Kent State Univ. Press, 1981.
       This massive listing of writing by and about
       Lovecraft is the most complete on the author to
       date, and will probably remain so for years to come.
       The primary material section includes all the sto-
       ries, articles, letters, and various contributions
       of Lovecraft that can be traced and definitely
       identified, as well as the many foreign trans-
       lations. The secondary material section presents
       virtually everything ever written about Lovecraft in
       all forms, from reviews and citations in reference
       works to periodical articles and book-length stud-
       ies. Material in this section is annotated and
       cross-referenced. Five indices provide access to
       the various contents of the volume. (MBT)

DICK LUPOFF (See F292)

ELIZABETH A. LYNN (See F106)

GEORGE MACDONALD (See also C12, E15, E18)

F179   McGraw, David John.   "Through the Land of the Seven
        Dimensions: A Philosophical Examination of Lilith."
        PS, 1 (1981), 81-90.
            Summary-explication of novel, ultimately relating
        to philosophical issues: "the nature and function of
        objects, the status of finite persons and the nature
        of space-time." (JS)

KATHERINE MACLEAN (See C13)

F180   MacLean, Katherine.   "The Expanding Mind."   In
        Fantastic Lives. Ed. Martin H. Greenberg. Carbon-
        dale: Southern Illinois Univ. Press, 1981, pp.
        79-101.
            In this autobiographical essay, MacLean tells of
        her growing interest in science fiction despite the
        active attempts of her family to prevent her from
        having any contact with it. Bibliography of her
        major science fiction works follows. (TPD)

EDWARD MAITLAND

F181   Seavey, Ormond, introd.   By and By: An Historical
        Romance of the Future. By Edward Maitland. Boston:
        Gregg Press, 1977.
            Though the future described in this work is
        filled with "imperialist racism, jingoism, sexism,
        and mysticism . . . its failures as prophecy and as
        novel make it the more interesting as a measure of
        mid-Victorian culture." (AT)

BARRY N. MALZBERG (See also I12)

F182   Malzberg, Barry N.   ". . . And a Chaser."   In Fan-
        tastic Lives. Ed. Martin H. Greenberg. Carbondale:
        Southern Illinois Univ. Press, 1981, pp. 102-17.
            Malzberg tells of gaining fame through writing
        science fiction and of his 1975 decision to leave
        the field. Bibliography of major science fiction
        works follows. (TPD)

F183   Stableford, Brian M.   "Insoluble Problems ('Foot-
        notes') to Barry Malzberg's Career in Science
        Fiction."   In Masters of Science Fiction. By Brian
        M. Stableford. San Bernardino, CA: Borgo Press,
        1981, pp. 24-31.
            It is not difficult, suggests Stableford, to
        understand why Malzberg has found science fiction
        such a frustrating genre in which to work. His
        purpose is quite opposite that of most readers, who
        prefer fiction that constitutes a single romp
        through a benevolent world, where obstacles are
        overcome and goodness wins out. Malzberg's work is
        of a different order. It is rooted in anxiety,

uncertainty, contradition. This poses a significant
problem--worse, because it defies a simple solution.
Sadly, Malzberg has failed to fashion a tolerable
compromise. (JME)

GEORGE R. R. MARTIN (See I13)

WILLIAM MAYNE (See C31)

JUDITH MERRIL (See C04)

A. MERRITT (See B27)

WALTER M. MILLER, JR.

F184 Spector, Judith A. "Walter Miller's A Canticle for
Leibowitz: A Parable for Our Time?" Midwest Quarterly, 22 (1981), 337-45.
  Spector uses passages from this science fiction
classic as correlations to the present-day debate
raging between scientists vs. nonscientists and
churchmen, the latter two denouncing the use of
nuclear energy, peaceful or otherwise. In his novel
Miller clearly hopes for cooperation between science
and religion to bring about a viable future. (PA)

NAOMI MITCHISON (See E20)

MICHAEL MOORCOCK

F185 Bilyeu, Richard. The Tanelorn Archives: A Primary
and Secondary Bibliography of the Works of Michael
Moorcock 1949-1979. Altona, Manitoba: Pandora's
Books, 1981.
  An extensive listing of over 1,300 items. Provides complete publishing history for Moorcock's
English-language books and stories. Additional
sections include the author's nonfiction, edito-
rials, reviews, fanzines, letters, comic books and
strips, music, films, manuscripts (in the Sterling
C. Evans Library, Texas A&M University), and
Moorcock-related material. Available in three
states: a trade paperback, a regular hardcover, and
a 250-copy edition numbered and signed by the
author. (MBT)

F186 Darlington, Andrew. "The Evolution of Michael
Moorcock." Dark Horizons, No. 22 (1981), pp. 4-10.
  An examination of Moorcock's literary development. Numerous influences in his work are traced,
particularly Edgar Rice Burroughs and Poul
Anderson's "The Broken Sword," as well as the Faust
myth, Biblical themes, and folklore. Several of
Moorcock's most important novels and creations such
as Elric, are discussed. Concludes that while his
best work defies categorization, he draws heavily on
traditional science fiction and fantasy themes such
as fantastic voyages, time travel, and sword and
sorcery. (JF)

F187   Platt, Charles, introd. The Condition of Muzak.   By
       Michael Moorcock. Boston: Gregg Press, 1978.
           Brief survey of all four Jerry Cornelius novels.
       Concludes that the last book is an epitaph for the
       lost generation of the 1960s. (AT)

WARD MOORE (See C04)

KENNETH MORRIS (See E28)

WILLIAM MORRIS (See C12, E18)

H. WARNER MUNN

F188   Bush, Laurence C. "The Realms of H. Warner Munn."
       The Romantist, No. 4-5 (1980-81), pp. 41-42.
           Discusses Munn's combining of Atlantean and
       Arthurian myths in his "Merlin's Ring" trilogy.
       (SE)

IRIS MURDOCH

F189   Winsor, Dorothy A. "Iris Murdoch and the Uncanny:
       Supernatural Events in The Bell."   Literature and
       Psychology, 13 (1980), 147-54.
           Concludes that through her use of the super-
       natural, Murdoch expresses a distrust of people's
       ability to maintain an adult, realistic basis for
       their actions. (PA)

RUTH NICHOLS (See C31)

WILLIAM F. NOLAN

F190   Elliot, Jeffrey. "Interview: William F. Nolan."
       FN, No. 33 (1981), pp. 10-13.
           Versatile writer Nolan discusses fantasy stories
       and screenplays. Mentions the relation of his work
       to Bradbury, historical research, and other sources
       of images. (JS)

ANDRE NORTON (See B28)

GEORGE ORWELL (See also C18)

F191   Hunter, Jefferson. "Orwell, Wells, and Coming Up
       for Air." Modern Philology, 78 (1980), 38-47.
           Demonstrates Wellsian influence on Orwell's
       prewar writing, especially Coming Up for Air, which
       predicts aerial bombardment of Britain in 1939.
       Argues that Wells's social novels, not his science
       fiction, had a stronger influence on Orwell. (JAG)

F192   Lewis, Peter. George Orwell: The Road to 1984. New
       York and London: Harcourt Brace Jovanovich, 1981.
           An illustrated biography and critical study which
       integrates the facts of Orwell's life and work into
       a unified pattern. (MBT)

ROBERT PALTOCK

F193   Bullen, A. H., introd. The Life & Adventures of
       Peter Wilkins. By Robert Paltock. Westport, CT:
       Hyperion Press, 1974.
            A brief recounting of the novel's publishing
       history and report of critical attitudes, plus a
       demonstration of Paltock's literary debt to Gul-
       liver's Travels and Robinson Crusoe. (AT)

MERVYN PEAKE

F194   Berkeley, Dee, and G. Peter Winnington. "Peake in
       Print." MPR, No. 13 (1981), pp. 8-35.
            An exhaustive, descriptive bibliography of
       Peake's in-print art and writing. (RCS)

F195   Bristow-Smith, Laurence. "A Critical Conclusion:
       The End of Titus Alone." MPR, No. 12 (1981), pp.
       10-13.
            An analysis of the conclusion of Titus Alone as
       the pivotal and climatic passage for the entire
       Gormenghast trilogy. (RCS)

F196   Greenland, Colin. "From Beowulf to Kafka: Mervyn
       Peake's 'Titus Alone.'" Foundation, No. 21 (1981),
       pp. 48-53.
            As an apt image of "the latter days," this final
       book of Peake's, though flawed, is so affective that
       readers have misunderstood and recoiled from its
       message. (DMH)

F197   -------. "From Beowulf to Kafka: The Difficulty of
       Titus Alone." MPR, No. 12 (1981), pp. 4-9.
            An assessment of the unrevised nature and prob-
       lems of Titus Alone and an answer to various
       scholars who have had difficulty with the novel.
       (RCS)

F198   Winnington, G. Peter (See F194)

F199   Winnington, G. Peter. "Editing Peake." MPR, No. 13
       (1981), pp. 2-7.
            Winnington comments on the significance of and
       quandaries involved with his textual modifications
       of the new Penguin, Methuen, and Overlook Press edi-
       tions of the Gormenghast trilogy. (RCS)

MARGE PIERCY (See also B21, D24, E14)

F200   Kress, Susan. "In and Out of Time: The Form of
       Marge Piercy's Novels." In Future Females. Ed.
       Marleen S. Barr. Bowling Green, OH: Bowling Green
       State Univ. Popular Press, 1981, pp. 109-22.
            Only in the carefully imagined futures made
       possible by science fiction forms does Piercy find a
       vehicle for presenting positive images of women.
       (TPD)

CHARLES PLATT (See F83, F136, F187)

EDGAR ALAN POE (See also C16, E16, E19)

F201   Kopley, Richard. "The Secret of Arthur Gordon Pym:
        The Text and the Source." Studies in American
        Fiction, 8 (1981), 203-18.
            Speculates on the nature of the "shrouded human
        figure" encountered by Pym in the Antarctic and its
        possible source in the journal of Antarctic explorer
        J. N. Reynolds. (JAG)

FREDERIK POHL (See D11, E09, H25)

GUSTAVUS W. POPE

F202   Moskowitz, Sam. "Gustavus W. Pope: Creator of 'The
        Scientific Romance.'" Introd. Journey to Mars. By
        Gustavus W. Pope. Westport, CT: Hyperion Press,
        1974.
            Demonstrates that Journey to Mars is a transition
        work between the schools of Jules Verne and Edgar
        Rice Burroughs; compares elements of Pope's work to
        H. Ride Haggard's She and Bulwer-Lytton's The Coming
        Race, and compares Pope's Mars to that of Burroughs.
        (AT)

THOMAS PYNCHON (See also C27, E17)

F203   Cullen, Robert Joseph. "Words and a Yarn: Language
        and Narrative Technique in the Works of Thomas
        Pynchon." Ph.D. dissertation, University of Cali-
        fornia, Los Angeles, 1981; DAI, 42: 1634A.
            Discusses the evolution of Pynchon's style toward
        the unique prose of Gravity's Rainbow. (PA)

F204   Gorman, Lawrence John. "Gravity's Rainbow: The
        Promise and Trap of Mythology." Ph.D. dissertation,
        Northern Illinois University, 1981; DAI, 42: 1630A.
            Argues that Gravity's Rainbow is in large part
        self-reflexive mythology in that it is a mythology
        detailing the often oppresive effects of mytholo-
        gies. (PA)

F205   Hite, Molly Patricia. "Ideas of Order in the Novels
        of Thomas Pynchon." Ph.D. dissertation, University
        of Washington, 1981; DAI, 42: 214A.
            This study of three works (V., The Crying of Lot
        49, and Gravity's Rainbow) examines Pynchon's fan-
        tasy worlds, concluding that they are complex and
        difficult but not incoherent. (PA)

F206   Kappel, Lawrence. "Psychic Geography in Gravity's
        Rainbow." Contemporary Literature, 21 (1980),
        225-51.
            According to Kappel, Pynchon has imagined a
        mythical region of adventure and magic, comparing
        the "Zone" (London in 1944 and Germany in 1945) to
        L. Frank Baum's Land of Oz. (JAG)

F207   Westervelt, Linda A.   "A Place Dependent on Our-
       selves: The Reader as System-Builder in Gravity's
       Rainbow."   Texas Studies in Language and Literature,
       22 (1980), 69-90.
          Explores the way in which Pynchon experiments
       with narrative voices, demonstrating that the "nar-
       rator Pynchon's" character and opinions are deliber-
       ately made difficult, if not impossible, for the
       reader to pinpoint.   (JAG)

       BILL RANSOM (See E02)

       MACK REYNOLDS

F208   Reynolds, Mack.   "Science Fiction and Socioeconom-
       ics."   In Fantastic Lives.   Ed. Martin H. Greenberg.
       Carbondale: Southern Illinois Univ. Press, 1981, pp.
       118-43.
          Reynolds fuses comment on his radical youth and
       his thirty years of free-lance writing, mainly of
       science fiction novels.   Bibliography of his major
       science fiction works follows.   (TPD)

F209   Stableford, Brian M.   "Utopia--And Afterwards:
       Socioeconomic Speculations in the Science Fiction of
       Mack Reynolds."   In Masters of Science Fiction.   By
       Brian M. Stableford.   San Bernardino, CA: Borgo
       Press, 1981, pp. 43-64.
          There is in Reynolds' fiction a "wide chasm"
       between the engaging ideas which he treats and his
       crude method of plotting.   This imbalance, maintains
       Stableford, is "the result of a compromise which he
       feels obliged to make in order to be sure that his
       work will be marketable."   Indeed, present market
       conditions make little provision for his unique
       brand of socioeconomic speculation.   Therefore, in
       order to treat such ideas, he is forced to fall back
       on "routine melodrama"--the kind which typifies the
       lower-strata of the marketplace.   (JME)

       W. H. RHODES

F210   Moskowitz, Sam.   "The Science Fiction Hoaxes of
       William Henry Rhodes."   Introd. Caxton's Book: A
       Collection of Essays, Poems, Tales and Sketches.   By
       W. H. Rhodes.   Ed. Daniel O'Connell.   Westport, CT:
       Hyperion Press, 1974.
          Brief biography of Rhodes, a recounting of the
       public reaction to his hoax, The Case of Summer-
       field, and a demonstration that Rhodes's hoaxes were
       part of a literary tradition begun by Richard Locke
       in The Moon Hoax and Poe in The Balloon Hoax.   (AT)

       KENNETH ROBESON [pseud. of Lester Dent]

F211   Farmer, Philip Jose.   Doc Savage: His Apocalyptic
       Life.   New York: Playboy, 1981 pbk.
          A "biography" of Lester Dent's fictional super

hero, who first appears in the <u>Doc Savage</u> magazine,
March 1933. Contains a list of the Doc Savage
stories. Reprint of 1973 Doubleday and 1975 Bantam
editions. (MBT)

VICTOR ROUSSEAU

F212   Del Rey, Lester. "A Neglected Masterpiece."
        Introd. <u>The Messiah of the Cylinder</u>. By Victor
        Rousseau. Westport,CT: Hyperion Press,1974.
            Claims the work is the first anti-utopia of
        political power, the true ancestor of Huxley and
        Orwell. (AT)

JOANNA RUSS (See also B20, C14, D19, D24)

F213   Delany, Samuel R., introd. <u>Alyx</u>. By Joanna Russ.
        Boston: Gregg Press, 1976.
            The Alyx stories raise the question of the rela-
        tionship between sword and sorcery and science
        fiction. Delany suspects that sword and sorcery may
        "express the archetypical underpinnings beneath the
        cognitively recomplicated surfaces we recognize as
        science fiction." (AT)

F214   Tobin, Jean, introd. <u>We Who Are About To...</u>. By
        Joanna Russ. Boston: Gregg Press, 1978.
            Compares Russ's narrator, the exile Nobody, to Le
        Guin's character Laia (Odo) and demonstrates Russ's
        use of science fiction "to explore new roles and
        relationships for women." (AT)

MARGARET ST. CLAIR

F215   St. Clair, Margaret. "Wight in Space: An Autobiog-
        raphical Sketch." In <u>Fantastic Lives</u>. Ed. Martin
        H. Greenberg. Carbondale: Southern Illinois Univ.
        Press, 1981, pp. 144-56.
            St. Clair faults science fiction for nurturing
        unrealistic expectations of a power-rich future and
        in other ways confesses to not being a science
        fiction fan. Bibliography of her major science
        works follows. (TPD)

ROD SERLING

F216   "Rod Serling: First Citizen of the Twilight Zone."
        <u>TZM</u> (April 1981), pp. 8-11.
            Biography of Serling, with post-1947 period
        recalled by his widow, Carol Serling. (SE)

GARRETT P. SERVISS

F217   Searles, A. Langley. "<u>A Columbus of Space</u>:
        Serviss's Most Prophetic Novel." Introd. <u>A
        Columbus of Space</u>. By Garrett P. Serviss.
        Westport, CT: Hyperion Press, 1974.

Brief biography of Serviss and a demonstration
that his novels combine a rousing adventure story
with remarkably prophetic extrapolations of scientific knowledge in the early twentieth century.
(AT)

F218 Wrzos, Joseph. "The Second Deluge: Serviss' Master-
work." Introd. The Second Deluge. By Garrett P.
Serviss. Westport, CT: Hyperion Press, 1974.
Brief biography of Serviss showing how he used
his passion for astronomy, his faith in reason and
science, and his criticisms of the world to tell the
story of a worldwide deluge set in the distant
future.

WILLIAM SHAKESPEARE

F219 Valli, Luigi. "Shakespeare and Fantasy: Modern
Theories and Interpretations of the Genre." Ph.D.
dissertation, Bowling Green State University, 1981;
DAI, 42: 4464A.
Examines modern theories of fantasy and the
fantastic and applies them to two of Shakespeare's
plays, A Midsummer Night's Dream and The Tempest.
(PA)

BOB SHAW

F220 Kincaid, Paul, and Geoff Rippington, eds. Bob Shaw.
British Science Fiction Writers, No. 1. Kent,
England: British Science Fiction Assoc., 1981 pbk.
The first volume of a projected series of book-
lets on leading British science fiction writers.
Contains a critical essay on Shaw by Brian Stable-
ford and a bibliography of Shaw's works by Mike
Ashley.

F221 Rippington, Geoff (See F220)

ROBERT SHECKLEY

F222 Powers, Richard Gid, introd. The 10th Victim. By
Robert Sheckley. Boston: Gregg Press, 1978.
This novel about boredom demonstrates Sheckley's
use of games theory. (AT)

F223 Schweitzer, Darrell. "An Interview with Robert
Sheckley." SFR, No. 40 (1981), pp. 7-9.
Sheckley discusses his position as fiction editor
at Omni, with special emphasis on the content and
character of the magazine, reader preferences and
tastes, magazine requirements and policies, and
favorite stories and features. Sheckley also
describes his own writing career, past and present
projects, recent trends in the genre, and magazine
publishing in general. (JME)

MARY SHELLEY (See also D06, E10)

F224   Conger, Syndy McMillen. "A German Ancestor for Mary
       Shelley's Monster: Kahlert, Schiller, and the Buried
       Treasure of Northanger Abbey." Philological
       Quarterly, 59 (1980), 216-32.
           Discusses the influence of German literature on
       English Gothic fiction, but more pointedly, shows
       the possible influence of Friedrich Schiller's work
       on Mary Shelley's creation of Frankenstein. (PA)

F225   Harvey, A. D. "Frankenstein and Caleb Williams."
       Keats Shelley Journal, 29 (1980), 21-27.
           Contends Mary Shelley did not conceive of
       Frankenstein as a prophecy of the new scientific era
       but rather as a Gothic horror novel. Also suggests
       that the novel's structure both parallels and re-
       verses the dramatic structure of Godwin's work,
       identifying the creature with Falkland and Victor
       Frankenstein with Caleb. (JAG)

F226   Reed, John R. "Will and Fate in Frankenstein."
       Bulletin of Research in the Humanities, 83 (1980),
       319-38.
           Discusses varying attitudes of the three nar-
       rators in the novel--Walton, Frankenstein, and Mary
       Shelley--towards the influence of free will and
       determinism on the events of the novel. (JAG)

F227   Sherwin, Paul. "Frankenstein: Creation as Catas-
       trophe." PMLA, 96 (1981), 883-903.
           Considers both the value and the limitations of a
       classical psychoanalytical reading of Shelley's
       novel. Ultimately such a reading fails to illu-
       cidate Frankenstein's role as the creator of the
       sublime artwork which both represents and eclipses
       that creator. (JAG)

       M. P. SHIEL

F228   Hartwell, David G., introd. The Purple Cloud. By
       M. P. Shiel. Boston: Gregg Press, 1977.
           Summary of Shiel's "future history" trilogy, The
       Last Miracle, The Lord of the Sea,and The Purple
       Cloud; analysis of The Purple Cloud as a Poesque
       post-catastrophe last man tale also influenced by
       Mary Shelley's The Last Man, by H. G. Wells, and by
       Nietzsche's superman theories. (AT)

       JOHN SHIRLEY (See I06)

       ROBERT SILVERBERG (See also F84, F263, I16)

F229   Dean, John. "The Sick Hero Reborn: Two Versions of
       the Philoctetes Myth." Comparative Literature
       Studies, 17 (1980), 334-40.
           Compares mythological content of Robert Silver-
       berg's Man in the Maze to the Sophoclean tragedy of

Philoctetes. In Silverberg's story, the wound that will not heal is the protagonist's telepathic ability to communicate his "soul"--the innermost workings of his heart and mind. (JAG)

F230 Elliot, Jeffrey M. "Robert Silverberg--Next Stop: Lord Valentine's Castle." P*S*F*Q, No. 5 (1981), pp. 18-24.
       Author Silverberg discusses his decision to resume writing and why he feels he was wrong when he said that commercial science fiction is no place for a serious writer. He describes his four-year hiatus from the field and how that period contributed to his growth, both as a writer and human being. (JME)

F231 Justice, Keith L. "Background and Checklist: Don Elliott/Robert Silverberg Erotic Fiction Titles." Megavore, No. 13 (1981), pp. 18-24.
       Background information on porno publishing in the 1959-65 period and specific details about the Elliott/Eliot/Silverberg books. Includes an in-progress checklist arranged by imprint and numerically by book number within the imprint groups. (MBT)

F232 Letson, Russell, introd. To Open the Sky. By Robert Silverberg. Boston: Gregg Press, 1977.
       Argues that the novel announces the themes of alienation and isolation which Silverberg explores in his later fiction. (AT)

F233 Stableford, Brian M. "The Metamorphosis of Robert Silverberg." In Masters of Science Fiction. By Brian M. Stableford. San Bernardino, CA: Borgo Press, 1981, pp. 32-42.
       Silverberg has been the most prolific science fiction writer of the past two decades. No less significant is the profound change which has characterized his writing over the past ten years. (JME)

CLIFFORD D. SIMAK

F234 Schweitzer, Darrell. "Clifford Simak." In Science Fiction Voices #5. Ed. Darrell Schweitzer. San Bernardino, CA: Borgo Press, 1981, pp. 48-55.
       Science fiction pioneer Simak responds to a wide variety of questions, including his attraction to the genre, his apprenticeship in the field, early writing attempts, working with editors, collaborations, and other assorted topics. He also discusses several of his best-known works, his special brand of science fiction, his place in the field, and the future of the genre. (JME)

KATHLEEN SKY (See I17)

GILBERT SORRENTINO

F235 Cioffi, Frank. "Gilbert Sorrentino's Science
      Fiction World in Mulligan Stew." Extrapolation, 22
      (1981), 140-45.
           An example of "metafiction," Mulligan Stew uses a
      deliberate artificial style based on pop culture to
      create a fantastic version of life in America--but
      one that is truer to our sense-bombarded reality
      than mimetic science fiction could be. (JS)

NORMAN SPINRAD (See also F02)

F236 Dahlin, Robert. "PW Interviews: Norman Spinrad."
      Publishers Weekly, 2 January 1981, pp. 8-9.
           The outspoken, irrepressible Spinrad expresses
      his irritation at the lack of serious consideration
      given science fiction by reviewers; warns publishers
      that the SFWA is a powerful community of writers
      prepared to hold out for "acceptable" contracts; and
      talks about his many diverse interests. (PA)

F237 Spinrad, Norman. "A Prince from Another Land." In
      Fantastic Lives. Ed. Martin H. Greenberg. Carbon-
      dale: Southern Illinois Univ. Press, 1981, pp.
      157-74.
           Spinrad discusses the theory behind his fiction
      with extended comment on George Clayton Jackson
      (co-author of Logan's Run), his own The Iron Dream
      and Passing Through the Flame, a mainstream novel
      about modern Hollywood. Bibliography of major
      science fiction works follows. (TPD)

BRIAN M. STABLEFORD (See also D27, F183, F209, F220,
F233, F269)

F238 Elliot, Jeffrey. "Interview: Brian Stableford."
      Starship, No. 42 (1981), 15-20.
           Questions covering Stableford's careers as
      academic (reporting on the low status of science
      fiction studies in Britain), critic (interested in
      the sociology of science fiction), and writer
      (trying to do something inside action-adventure
      formulas). (JS)

OLAF STAPLEDON (See also C18)

F239 Huntington, John. "Olaf Stapledon and the Novel
      About the Future." Contemporary Literature, 22
      (1981), 345-65.
           Attempts to show how, in the futuristic novel
      Last and First Men, Stapledon achieved a form unique
      in literature through the use of the dialectical
      process. (PA)

F240 McCarthy, Patrick A. "Star Maker: Olaf Stapledon's
      Divine Tragedy." SFS, 8 (1981), 266-79.

A chapter from McCarthy's 1982 Twayne book on
Stapledon describing the familiar Swiftian and
Dantesque narrative pattern of this hugely ambitious
work. (DMH)

FRANK R. STOCKTON

F241   Golemba, Henry L. <u>Frank R. Stockton</u>. Twayne United
        States Authors, No. 374. Boston: Twayne, 1981.
            Attempts to synthesize Stockton's personal ex-
        perience with his art. Examines his relationship
        with the publishing industry, his audience, and his
        fan clubs. The first extended examination of
        Stockton's literary output. Primary and secondary
        bibliographies. (MBT)

BRAM STOKER (See also C33)

F242   Blinderman, Charles S. "Vampurella: Darwin and
        Count Dracula." <u>Massachusettes Review</u>, 21 (1980),
        411-28.
            An imaginative analysis implying that <u>Dracula</u> is
        an expression of Darwinian materialism in its var-
        ious themes: e.g., the assimilation of one being by
        another as the kinship of protoplasmic life, or
        identifying Count Dracula as the Social Darwinian
        superman, "the ultimate parasitic degenerate," the
        end product of the evolutionary process. (JAG)

F243   Faig, Kenneth W., Jr. "About Bram." <u>The Romantist</u>,
        No. 4-5 (1980-81), pp. 39-40.
            Outline of Stoker's life and a valuable discus-
        sion of each of his books which, except for <u>Dracula</u>,
        are little-known. Checklist of first English and
        American editions and selective secondary bibliog-
        raphy. (SE)

F244   Griffin, Gail B. "'Your Girls That You All Love Are
        Mine': <u>Dracula</u> and the Victorian Male Sexual Imagi-
        nation." <u>International Journal of Women's Studies</u>,
        3 (1980), 454-65.
            Argues that the threat in <u>Dracula</u> is not the
        predatory male sexuality of the Count, but the more
        vivid sexuality of his female surrogates, the trio
        at the castle and Lucy Westenra, who became "mon-
        sters" by perverted maternal instincts. (JAG)

F245   Hatlen, Burton. "The Return of the Repressed/Op-
        pressed in Bram Stoker's <u>Dracula</u>." <u>Minnesota
        Review</u>, 15 (1980), 80-97.
            Examines <u>Dracula</u> as subject/example of Marxist
        criticism of romance. Sees Dracula as a symbol of
        social, racial, economic, and sexual "otherness"
        which the Victorian bourgeoisie had to repress.
        (JAG)

PETER STRAUB

F246   Gregory, Jay. "Peter Straub: 'I Looked Into My
       Imagination and That's What I Found.'" TZM (May
       1981), pp. 13-16.
          Interview with the popular horror novelist.
       Biographical recollections, including Straub's early
       reading. Straub discusses his theories of horror
       fiction and the creation of his works. (SE)

W. J. STUART

F247   Milicia, Joseph, introd. Forbidden Planet. By W.
       J. Stuart. Boston: Gregg Press, 1978.
          Compares the novel version to the film and to
       Shakespeare's The Tempest. Perceives Forbidden
       Planet as a competent novel in some ways superior to
       the film but not an outstanding science fiction
       novel in its own right. (AT)

THEODORE STURGEON (See also C04, F38)

F248   Delany, Samuel R., introd. The Cosmic Rape and "To
       Marry Medusa." By Theodore Sturgeon. Boston: Gregg
       Press, 1977.
          Compares Sturgeon, master of near-future science
       fiction, with Alfred Bester, master of far-future
       science fiction, and recounts the impact on the
       science fiction community and on Delany of
       Sturgeon's rewriting of the story "Maturity." Also
       compares the details of Sturgeon's two versions of
       The Cosmic Rape. (AT)

F249   Diskin, Lahna. Theodore Sturgeon. Starmont
       Reader's Guide, No. 7. Mercer Island, WA: Starmont
       House, 1981 pbk.
          This study guide consists of a chronology of
       Sturgeon's life and works, a biocritical intro-
       duction, chapters on the novels and stories, and
       both primary and secondary bibliographies. The
       first comprehensive survey of Sturgeon. (MBT)

F250   Hayles, N. B. "An Imperfect Art: Competing Patterns
       in More Than Human." Extrapolation, 22 (1981),
       13-24.
          Finds conflict between ideas and characterization
       in Sturgeon's most celebrated novel: characters
       strain to grow in power and responsibility, develop-
       ing from childishness to maturity and from isolation
       to gestalt; however, homo gestalt as described by
       Sturgeon doesn't take full advantage of "parent-
       child dynamic." As a result, the novel is an
       interesting failure. (JS)

F251   Menger, Lucy. Theodore Sturgeon. Recognitions
       series. New York: Frederick Ungar, 1981.
          In this examination of Sturgeon's work and phi-
       losophy, the author explores the changes in his

writing through the years, his precedent-setting use
of sex, and his commitment to opening his readers'
minds. Includes a list of criticism and a selected
Sturgeon bibliography. Also issued in paperback.
(MBT)

JAMES TIPTREE, JR. [pseud. of Alice Sheldon] (See
D24)

J. R. R. TOLKIEN (See also C18, E03-07, E21, E22)

F252   Barkley, Christine. "Predictability and Wonder:
        Familiarity and Recovery in Tolkien's World."
        Mythlore, No. 27 (1981), pp. 16-18.
            Tolkien gives a sense of predictable order in his
        works, yet he creates recognition of fresh (or
        hitherto overlooked) wonder in experience. (JS)

F253   Crabbe, Katharyn. J. R. R. Tolkien. New York:
        Frederick Ungar, 1981.
            An assessment of Tolkien's achievement which
        explores the extent to which his novels and stories
        may be seen as Christian apologetics. A compact
        introduction to Tolkien's work. Also issued in
        paperback. (MBT)

F254   Helms, Randel. Tolkien and the Silmarils. Boston:
        Houghton Mifflin, 1981.
            An analysis of The Silmarillion which discusses
        the sources of the work, its major themes, and its
        relationship to Tolkien's other writings. (MBT)

F255   Hodge, James L. "Tolkien: Formulas of the Past."
        Mythlore, No. 29 (1981), pp. 15-18.
            Shows Tolkien echoing verbal formulas from tradi-
        tional tales and his acceptance of the role of oral
        storyteller and sage. (JS)

F256   Isaacs, Neil D., and Rose A. Zimbardo, eds.
        Tolkien: New Critical Perspectives. Lexington, KY:
        Univ. Press of Kentucky, 1981.
            Thirteen reprinted and original essays survey
        recent Tolkien scholarship with emphasis on The Lord
        of the Rings. [Contents not annotated.] (MBT)

F257   Miller, Miriam Y. "The Green Sun: A Study of Color
        in J. R. R. Tolkien's The Lord of the Rings."
        Mythlore, No. 26 (1981), pp. 3-11.
            Tolkien's effects are created by using primary
        hues of a relatively few colors: thematically, light
        and dark suggest good and evil; colors sometimes
        serve as heraldic signs of identity for places and
        people (and as an indication of moral condition);
        Tolkien permits the reader to visualize the action
        in primary, pure colors. (JS)

F258   West, Richard C. Tolkien Criticism: An Annotated
        Checklist. Rev. ed. Kent, OH; Kent State Univ.
        Press, 1981.

First published in 1970, this revised edition
documents the enormous amount of Tolkien scholarship
published during the decade of the 1970s. Section 1
lists Tolkien's published works; Section 2 (the main
body of the volume) consists of critical and scholarly writings on Tolkien and his work; Section 3 is
a checklist of book reviews; and Section 4 consists
of several indexes designed to assist the reader in
the use of the other sections. All entries are
annotated. The volume includes "everything related
to Tolkien's scholarly and fictive work that is
definitely of real importance, from the time he
began publishing in the 1920s down through the
greater part of 1980." The volume excludes translations of Tolkien's work, adaptations of Tolkien
into other media and related articles, most news-
paper articles, and material from most fanzines
because such publications are generally not indexed
nor collected. A necessary reference tool for
Tolkien scholars. (MBT)

F259   Zimbardo, Rose A. (See F256)

WILSON TUCKER

F260   Schweitzer, Darrell. "Wilson Tucker." In Science
Fiction Voices #5. San Bernardino, CA: Borgo Press,
1981, pp. 55-60.
       Tucker displays the wit and wisdom for which he
is known, describing his attraction to science
fiction, his involvement in fandom, his move from
the amateur to professional ranks, and several of
his best-known works. (JME)

MARK TWAIN

F261   Winters, Donald E. "The Utopianism of Survival:
Bellamy's Looking Backward and Twain's A Connecticut
Yankee." American Studies, 21 (1980), pp. 23-28.
       Demonstrates Twain's fascination with Looking
Backward and its possible influence on Connecticut
Yankee. In both novels, the protagonists are
"survivors" who offer utopian solutions to their
respective societies' ills. (JAG)

A. E. VAN VOGT

F262   van Vogt, A. E. "My Life Was My Best Science Fiction Story." In Fantastic Lives. Ed. Martin H.
Greenberg. Carbondale: Southern Illinois Univ.
Press, 1981, pp. 175-215.
       Van Vogt comments on his productive decade, his
association with L. Ron Hubbard and dianetics, and
his current interests. Bibliography of his major
science fiction works follows. (TPD)

JACK VANCE

F263 Silverberg, Robert, introd. Eyes of the Overworld.
      By Jack Vance. Boston: Gregg Press, 1977.
      Compares Eyes of the Overworld with its companion
      work, The Dying Earth. (AT)

JOHN VARLEY (See also B05)

F264 Hall, Melissa Mia. "Riding the Dangers." Starship,
      No. 42 (1981), pp. 21-22.
      Interview-essay on John Varley, discussing treat-
      ment of gender in his fiction, inspiration of Titan
      and its sequels, with random comments on his writing
      career. (JS)

THEA VON HARBOU

F265 Rogers, Deborah C. (See F266)

F266 Rogers, Ivor A., and Deborah C. Rogers, introd. The
      Rocket to the Moon. By Thea Von Harbou. Boston:
      Gregg Press, 1977.
      Explains the significance of the characters'
      names and the author's adherence to the German
      literary tradition. Also argues that this is a
      better book than Metropolis, although the Metropolis
      movie is superior to Die Frau im Mond, the movie
      version of Rocket To the Moon. (AT)

KURT VONNEGUT, JR.

F267 Reilly, Charles. "Two Conversations with Kurt
      Vonnegut." College Literature, 7 (1980), 1-29.
      Reilly gives us two interviews with Vonnegut,
      three years apart, as part of a series of interviews
      with living American authors. Of interest is Von-
      negut's story of Farmer's Venus on the Half-Shell.
      (JAG)

F268 Rose, Ellen Cronan. "It's All a Joke : Science
      Fiction in Kurt Vonnegut's The Sirens of Titan."
      Literature and Psychology, 29 (1979), 160-68.
      Using Freud's analysis of techniques of joking,
      Rose contends that Vonnegut jokes around with sci-
      ence fiction elements and that he is at his best in
      The Sirens of Titan. (JAG)

F269 Stableford, Brian M. "Locked in the Slaughterhouse:
      The Novels of Kurt Vonnegut." In Masters of Science
      Fiction. By Brian M. Stableford. San Bernardino,
      CA: Borgo Press, 1981, pp. 15-23.
      Maintains that what makes Vonnegut outstanding
      among his writing peers is not that he has exper-
      ienced the horrors of Dresden, nor that he was
      blessed with some superhuman talent, nor that he has
      cleverly seduced the critics; rather, it is that he
      has endeavored to fashion a world view compatable

with what he has known and seen, and to draw on that
world view in a fictional milieu. His answers to
life's most vexing questions seem both ironic and
grotesque. They are not, however, idealistic whim-
sies nor juvenile satires. They reflect bitter
comedy, creative energy, and moral fury, qualities
which are powerful and real. (JME)

KARL EDWARD WAGNER (See also I20)

F270 Elliot, Jeffrey. "Interview: Karl Edward Wagner."
      FN, No. 38 (1981), pp. 17-22, 34.
        Discusses personal background and purpose in
woriting, along with early career as a writer. First
of two parts. (JS)

F271 ------. "Interview: Karl Edward Wagner." FN, No.
      39 (1981), pp. 12-17, 21.
        More on attraction of his hero-villain Kane and
on approaches to writing. (JS)

DIANE WAKOSKI (See E14)

IAN WATSON (See I21)

STANLEY G. WEINBAUM

F272 Weinbaum, Stanley G. "An Autobiographical Sketch of
      Stanley G. Weinbaum." In A Martian Odyssey and
      Other Science Fiction Tales: The Collected Short
      Stories of Stanley G. Weinbaum. By Stanley G.
      Weinbaum. Westport, CT: Hyperion Press, 1974.
        Argues that science fiction too often ignores the
fact that scientists describe but do not interpret
actions and that most writers fail to take advantage
of science fiction's freedom to criticize the human
condition. (AT)

MANLY WADE WELLMAN

F273 Schweitzer, Darrell. "Amazing Interview: An Inter-
      view with Manly Wade Wellman." Amazing (March
      1981), pp. 122-26.
        Wellman discusses his childhood in Angola and how
it may have influenced his writing. Also mentioned
are editors, folklore, Hollywood adaptations, and
his own work. (TWH)

H. G. WELLS (See also C33, D07, F63, F118, F191)

F274 Huntington, John. "Thinking by Opposition: The
      'Two-World' Structure in H. G. Wells's Short Fic-
      tion." SFS, 8 (1981), 240-54.
        Exploration of a fundamental structural element
in all of Wells's early fiction. (DMH)

F275 -------. "Wells's Time Traveller: An Unreliable
      Narrator?" Extrapolation, 22 (1981), 117-26.

       Readers must not trust the Time Traveller's
  statement that Morlocks are mentally degenerate,
  since his reactions are based on unthinking physical
  revulsion and on snobbish preference for the pretty
  Eloi. Actually, the Time Traveller is an unreliable
  observer, as are several other of Wells's early
  narrators. (JS)

F276 Lake, David. "The Whiteness of Griffin and H. G.
      Wells's Images of Death, 1897-1914." SFS, 8 (1981),
      12-18.
           Discussion of the ambivalent symbol of whiteness
      in Wells's work up to the eve of World War I, with
      emphasis on Griffin's albinism in The Invisible Man
      as well as the Melvillian equation of whiteness with
      death and then upon Wells's change in the use of the
      image as he becomes more utopian. (DMH)

F277 McConnell, Frank. The Science Fiction of H. G.
      Wells. Science-Fiction Writers. New York: Oxford
      Univ. Press, 1981.
           After presenting the details of Wells's life,
      McConnell offers a broad overview of his work, with
      emphasis on the five major "scientific romances"
      through which Wells exercised his greatest influ-
      ence: The Time Machine, The Invisible Man, The
      Island of Dr. Moreau, The War of the Worlds, and The
      First Men in the Moon, all of which appeared between
      1895 and 1901. McConnell also discusses Wells's
      later work, including his important ventures into
      history writing and social theory. Treats Wells as
      a major literary figure, showing the importance of
      his background to an understanding of his work. A
      chronology of his life, a checklist of major writ-
      ings, and a critical bibliography conclude the
      volume. Also issued in paperback. (MBT)

F278 Mackerness, E. D. "Zola, Wells, and °The Coming
      Beast.'" SFS, 8 (1981), 143-48.
           A suggestion that a more "subtle affiliation"
      than with Verne helps to describe the imaginative
      power in Wells's science fiction; the parallel with
      Zola on the topic of social Darwinism is developed
      with a focus on Germinal (1885) and The Time Machine
      (1895). (DMH)

F279 Parrinder, Patrick, and Robert M. Philmus, eds. H.
      G. Wells's Literary Criticism. Totowa, NJ and
      Brighton, England: Barnes & Noble and Harvester
      Press, 1980.
           A collection of the best of Wells's literary
      criticism, some of which has never been previously
      identified. The essays and reviews are arranged
      into five categories covering a variety of subjects
      and writers. (MBT)

F280 Philmus, Robert M. (See also F279)

F281   -------. "The Satiric Ambivalence of <u>The</u> <u>Island of</u>
<u>Dr. Moreau</u>." <u>SFS</u>, 8 (1981), 2-11.
        A comparison of an early draft of this satire
with the published version in order to show the
development of Wells's Swiftian satire from earlier
more sublime intentions that were modeled after <u>Dr.</u>
<u>Jekyll and Mr. Hyde</u>. (DMH)

F282   Scafella, Frank. "The White Sphinx and <u>The Time</u>
<u>Machine</u>." <u>SFS</u>, 8 (1981), 255-65.
        A suggestion that the novel is an allegorical
rendering of the fable of Oedipus and the Sphinx as
Francis Bacon interpreted that fable with regard to
the predicament of the scientist in the modern
world. (DMH)

F283   Scheick, William J.   "Toward the Ultra-SF Novel: H.
G. Wells's <u>Star Begotten</u>." <u>SFS</u>, 8 (1981), 19-25.
        Though hardly known now, this 1937 novel was
apparently viewed by Wells as the culmination of his
evolutionary efforts toward a better "scientific
romance" or science fiction novel as he radically
adapts concepts from his earlier science fiction,
such as alien invasion, as well as develops the
narrative techniques in an evolutionary way. (DMH)

F284   Simmons, Harvey G. "H. G. Wells as Futurologist."
<u>English Studies in Canada</u>, 6 (1980), 212-31.
        In Wells's early science fiction novels and later
nonfiction writings, Simmons believes that Wells
took seriously the task of predicting the future and
felt deeply about the importance of educating the
public to look into the future and think about the
social problems of his age. (JAG)

T. H. WHITE

F285   Nelson, Marie. "Bird Language in T. H. White's <u>The</u>
<u>Sword in the Stone</u>." <u>Mythlore</u>, No. 28 (1981), pp.
35-37.
        White uses different styles to characterize
different animals encountered by the young Arthur.
(JS)

KATE WILHELM

F286   Wood, Susan, introd. <u>The Mile-Long Spaceship</u>. By
Kate Wilhelm. Boston: Gregg Press, 1980.
        Demonstrates that Wilhelm is a writer who defies
genre labels by analyzing her work to show that her
primary focus is on inner, not outer, space, the
"delusions, obsessions, the workings and malfunc-
tionings of the human mind." (AT)

CHARLES WILLIAMS (See also E03-07, E11)

F287   Beare, Rhona. "Charles Williams and the Stone."
<u>Mythlore</u>, No. 29 (1981), p. 34.

Background of the jewel that is the focus of
action in <u>Many Dimensions</u>. (JS)

F288   Carter-Day, Deborah. "°Coinherence' and °The Ter-
rible Good': A Soul's Journey to Awareness and
Responsibility." <u>Mythlore</u>, No. 26 (1981), pp.
27-30.
Discusses purgatorial experience of dead central
character in <u>All Hallows Eve</u>, who must overcome past
isolation and insensitivity to prevent Evil in the
realm of the living. (JS)

F289   Howard, Thomas. "Granting Charles Williams His
Donee." <u>Mythlore</u>, No. 28 (1981), pp. 13-14.
Lists Williams' deviations from traditional
English novel, but echoes Henry James in insisting
that the reader must grant the novelist his chosen
starting point, whatever it is; proper criticism
only concerns how well the writer uses his "given."
(JS)

F290   McClatchey, J. "Praise and Christian Unity in <u>War
in Heaven</u>." <u>Mythlore</u>, No. 27 (1981), pp. 19-21.
The strength to resist evil comes from habit of
Christian praise. The active force of the grail
symbolizes and confirms the unity the characters
have already practiced. (JS)

JACK WILLIAMSON

F291   Davidson, Larry (See F292)

F292   Lupoff, Dick, and Larry Davidson. "Interview with
Jack Williamson." <u>Rigel Science Fiction</u> (Fall
1981), pp. 28-33.
Williamson discusses his long career as a writer,
his experiences with various editors and other
writers, and plans for future work. (TWH)

F293   Luserke, Uwe. "Jack Williamson Bibliography."
<u>Megavore</u>, No. 13 (1981), pp. 29-41.
A chronological listing of Williamson's first
printings, as well as a complete listing of books
published through October 1978. Only the appearance
of the first part is listed for serialized stories.
(MBT)

F294   Schweitzer, Darrell. "Jack Williamson." In <u>Science
Fiction Voices #5</u>. San Bernardino, CA: Borgo Press,
1981, pp. 60-64.
Williamson examines the state of science fiction
in the 1920s, public acceptance of the genre, market
considerations and constraints, early science fiction magazines, the development of fandom, and the
contributions of John Campbell and Hugo Gernsback.
A number of other disparate topics are also discussed. (JME)

F295   Wilgus, Neal. "An Interview with Jack Williamson."
<u>SFR</u>, No. 38 (1981), pp. 26-29.

Williamson explores a wide variety of topics, including the impact of H. G. Wells on his life and work; his popular novelette, "With Folded Hands"; the meanings and messages of his major works; his much-acclaimed novel, Darker Than You Think; the academic acceptance of science fiction; the meaning and impact of science fiction awards. (JME)

F296   Willis, Joseph A. "The Quiet Master." Megavore, No. 13 (1981), pp. 26-29.
        Brief biography focused on career. (MBT)

ROBERT ANTON WILSON

F297   Elliot, Jeffrey. "Interview: Robert Anton Wilson." Starship, No. 41 (1981), 15-22.
        Covers writing career and expansive, bubbling interests in pop culture and ideology. (JS)

F298   Gengle, Dean. "Interview: Robert Anton Wilson." Future Life, No. 29 (1981), pp. 19-21.
        The author of Schrodinger's Cat and Illuminatus exposes the world wide conspiracy. (MBT)

GENE WOLFE (See also C35)

F299   Gordon, Joan. "An Interview with Gene Wolfe." SFR, No. 38 (1981), pp. 18-22.
        Wolfe explores a wide range of concerns, among them his early childhood, belief systems (religious and political), his beginnings as a writer, literary influences, his working regimen, favorite writers, academic criticism, assessment of the genre, personal goals and ambitions. (JME)

PHILIP WYLIE

F300   Bendau, Clifford P. Still Worlds Collide: Philip Wylie and the End of the American Dream. San Bernardino, CA: Borgo Press, 1980.
        A general survey of Wylie's writings, which range over many areas, including pulp science fiction, social diatribe, fantasy, romantic satire, mysteries, and warnings against the coming nuclear holocaust. (MBT)

CHELSEA QUINN YARBRO

F301   Elliot, Jeffrey. "Interview: Chelsea Quinn Yarbro." FN No. 43 (1981), pp. 10-15, 30.
        Concerns of a beginning writer whose interest in history and feminism enter her work very strongly. (JS)

EUGENE ZAMIATIN

F302   Mihailovich, Vasa D. "Appendix: Critics on Evgeny Zamyatin." In We. By Eugene Zamiatin. Trans. Gregory Zilboorg. Boston: Gregg Press, 1975.

A brief survey of Zamiatin's life and works, discussion of major critical judgment about him, and suggested topics for further research. (AT)

F303   Pitcher, Edward W. R.   "That Web of Symbols in Zamyatin's We." Extrapolation, 22 (1981), 252-61.
A careful analysis of conflict in the central character, D-503, in terms of fire (representing the natural world) and water (state). Concludes that neither side is purely desirable. "Thus D-503's dilemma is the human dilemma; we cannot opt for one or the other side of the polarized position in the novel." (JS)

F304   Rudy, Peter, introd. We. By Eugene Zamiatin. Trans. Gregory Zilboorg. Boston: Gregg Press, 1975.
Demonstrates the relevance of We, both at publication and at present, and argues that Zamiatin's theory "that most men believe their freedom to be more than a fair exchange for a high level of material happiness" has not yet been fully treated. (AT)

GEORGE ZEBROWSKI

F305   Zebrowski, George.   "The Profession of Science Fiction, 25: Perfecting Visions, Slaying Cynics." Foundation, No. 23 (1981), pp. 44-64.
In the interview format (conducted by Jeffrey M. Elliot), Zebrowski talks about his life and his methods of writing, with emphasis on the mixed critical reception of Macrolife. (DMH)

ROGER ZELANY (See also C26, D03)

F306   Thompson, W. B. "Interview: Roger Zelany." Future Life, No. 25 (1981), pp. 40-42.
The author of such novels as Lord of Light talks about his work and his life. (MBT)

F307   Thurston, Robert, introd. Today We Choose Faces.   By Roger Zelany. Boston: Gregg Press, 1978.
Demonstrates that Zelany "has obtained stunning narrative results by considering the links between and among detective fiction, Shakespearian and ancient Greek dramas, religious epics, and the important dilemmas that continue to trouble generations of humankind." (AT)

G. Art

G01   DiFate, Vincent. "Sketches." _Starship_, No. 41
       (1981), pp. 42-43.
           Shows how visual motifs are used to reinforce
       themes (especially by symbolic enclosures) in
       science fiction films such as _The Thing_, _The Day the
       Earth Stood Still_, and _The Manchurian Candidate_.
       (JS)

G02   -------. "Sketches: Tantalizing Images." _Starship_,
       No. 42 (1981), pp. 29-31.
           Mass market paperbacks have covers that use genre
       icons to attract buyers. This is not easy to do in
       science fiction, since symbols--such as robots--can
       take many forms. Links to basic attraction of
       science fiction: the fact that "it has no limits, no
       finite patterns, no unalterable axioms." (JS)

G03   Di Lauro, Stephen. "100 Years of Fantasy
       Illustration." _TZM_ (June 1981), pp. 36-41.
           Brief discussions of Dore, Beardsley, Sime,
       Rackham, W. Heath Robinson, Frank R. Paul, Max
       Ernst, Stephen Lawrence, Virgil Finlay, Rick
       Griffin, Lee Brown Coye, and Edward Gorey. (SE)

G04   Kalashnikova, Irina. "An Artist and His Space
       Fantasies." _Soviet Life_ (April 1981), pp. 50-52.
           Moldavian artist Mikhail Greku began painting
       space fantasies after participating in the inter-
       national symposium, _Space in Pictorial Art, 1973_.
       His creative imagination is often sparked by the
       types of paints he is using; thus his works have a
       limited range of colors but demonstrate diversified
       combinations of texture. (PA)

G05   McCarthy, Shawna. "Wayne D. Barlowe." _IASFM_ (March
       1981), pp. 68-71.
           Biography of the well-known science fiction
       artist, his influences, and his ways of working.
       (TWH)

G06   Miesel, Sandra. "An Interview with Michael Whelan."
       SFR, No. 41 (1981), pp. 26-31.
           Artist Whelan explores a host of topics, among
       them his attraction to science fiction, the appeal
       of art, his formal training, major influences, use
       of models, the state of the field, and much more.
       (JME)

G07   Mitchell, Elizabeth. "Artist Profile: Frank Borth."
      IASFM (June 1981), pp. 88-91.
          Biography and career of the science fiction
      illustrator. (TWH)

H. Media: Film, TV, Radio

(See also G01, J02, J09)

H01   Ackerman, Forrest J. (See H35)

H02   Asherman, Alan. The Star Trek Compendium. New
        York: Simon & Schuster, 1981.
            A gold mine of information for Star Trek fans,
        containing photography and production details,
        technical matters, series concepts and continuity,
        symbolism and trivia, episode titles, discussion of
        plots, career and biographical information on actors
        and production personnel. (MBT)

H03   Carroll, Noel. "Nightmare and the Horror Film: The
        Symbolic Biology of Fantastic Beings." Film Quar-
        terly, 34 (Spring 1981), 16-25.
            Analyzes the manner in which the imagery of
        horror films corresponds to that of a nightmare, and
        focuses on horrific creatures, or what the author
        terms the "symbolic biologies." (PA)

H04   Dowling, Terry, and George Mannix. "Peter Weir--
        Master of Unease." Science Fiction, 3 (1981), 7-27.
            An interview with a writer and director who is
        characterized as "Australia's most provocative and
        original film-maker," followed by a checklist of
        films, many of which are based on short stories by
        Weir or have been written by Weir. (DMH)

H05   Gagne, Paul R. "Science Fiction Typographics."
        Cinefantastique, 10 (Spring 1981), 36-41.
            Describes how animation, graphics, and imagina-
        tive typography are used in advertising or credits
        for genre films. (JS)

H06   Gallagher, Steve. "Blind Man's Movies." Vector,
        No. 105 (1981), pp. 7-14.
            Discusses radio science fiction and his own
        experience with the field. While radio drama is
        declining it provides opportunities for science
        fiction stories and is an ideal medium. (JF)

H07   Gittleman, Sol. "Fritz Lang's Metropolis and Georg
        Kaiser's Gas I: Film, Literature and the Crisis of
        Technology." Unterrichtspraxis, 12, No. 2 (1980),
        27-30.

Demonstrates that Lang's film reveals the evils
of technology by using a high level of emotionalism.
The film is both antilabor and anticapitalist.
(JAG)

H08   Goldsmith, Marlene Herbert. "Video Values Educa-
tion: Star Trek as a Modern Myth." Ph.D. diss.
University of Minnesota, 1981; DAI, 42: 4979A.
Because commercial television is the "common
school" of America this thesis analyzes a major TV
series and finds that, although made in the 1960s
and still widely shown today, Star Trek reflects a
1950s attitude. The question is then raised con-
cerning the desirability of allowing private owner-
ship of a medium that functions as a nation's "common school." (PA)

H09   Harryhausen, Ray. Film Fantasy Scrapbook. 3rd ed.
San Diego: A. S. Barnes, 1981, pbk.
Revised from the 1972 and 1974 editions, this
lightly expanded version is illustrated with posters
and photos covering every facet of Harryhausen's
career, and the text offers insights into production
techniques. This edition features new chapters on
Sinbad and the Eye of the Tiger and Clash of the
Titans. (MBT)

H10   Jones, Alan. "The Terror Film Career of Pete Walker." Dark Horizons, No. 23 (1981), pp. 3-7.
An introduction to the horror films of one of
Britain's most successful film directors. Each film
is discussed briefly in chronological order. (JF)

H11   Jones, Stephen. "Good Omens: An Interview with
Richard Donner." Dark Horizons, No. 24 (1981), pp.
14-20, 32.
Donner tells how he became a film director and
discusses his work on The Twilight Zone, The Omen,
and Superman, as well as future projects. (JF)

H12   Kagarlitski, Julius. "The Fantastic in Theatre and
Cinema." Extrapolation, 22 (1981), 5-12.
Sees both science fiction and fantasy as variations of the fantastic. Film, however, is like the
novel, capable of being fantastic throughout. (JS)

H13   King, Stephen. "Why We Crave Horror Movies."
Playboy (January 1981), pp. 150-54, 237-46.
We crave horror movies, says King, because we all
share a certain insanity that must be fed in order
to keep us civilized. In his urbane manner, King
develops his theme through a discussion of such
films as Night of the Living Dead, The Thing, The
Amityville Horror, The Stepford Wives, and Carrie.
He also discusses the horror film in its sociologi-
cal context. (PA)

H14   Lankin, Alan. "Science Fiction on the Dial." <u>IASFM</u>
       (September 1981), pp. 18-21.
           A report on the revival of productions of science
       fiction as radio drama, with emphasis on <u>Star Wars</u>
       and <u>Hitchhiker's Guide to the Galaxy</u>, analyzing why
       one fails while the other succeeds in this medium.
       (TWH)

H15   Leggett, Paul. "The Filmed Fantasies of Terrance
       Fisher." <u>Christianity Today</u>, 25 (January 1981),
       32-33.   .
           A tribute to British filmmaker Fisher whose
       fantasy films (<u>Dracula</u>, <u>Curse of the Werewolf</u>, <u>The
       Devil Rides Out</u>, and others) portray a Christian
       philosophy of evil. (PA)

H16   McCarty, John. <u>Splatter Movies: Breaking the Last
       Taboo</u>. Albany, NY: FantaCo Enterprises, 1981 pbk.
           A heavily-illustrated survey of this subspecies
       of the horror film. Commentary explores the roots
       of the splatter movie to its place in contemporary,
       discussing twenty or thirty films along the way.
       (MBT)

H17   Mank, Gregory William. <u>It's Alive! The Classic
       Cinema Saga of Frankenstein</u>. San Diego: A. S.
       Barnes, 1981 pbk.
           Chronicles the complete story of Universal
       Studio's monster saga. Each chapter is devoted to
       one of the eight films, beginning with the 1931
       release of <u>Frankenstein</u> and ending with the 1948
       spoof, <u>Abbott and Costello Meet Frankenstein</u>.
       Detailed credits, a full synopsis of each movie, and
       a production history for each film. A "Denouement"
       chapter covers the fates of various actors, direc-
       tors, and others after the series ended in 1948. A
       final chapter, "Further Frankenstein," summarizes
       some of the more recent Frankenstein movies inspired
       by the Universal series. A Biographical Appendix
       presents profiles of twenty-three of the most cele-
       brated veterans of the series. (MBT)

H18   Mannix, George (See H04)

H19   Martin, Robert. "Donner as Filmmaker: A Flair for
       the Larger-Than-Life." <u>TZM</u> (July 1981), pp. 53-56.
           A review of director Richard Donner's career.
       (SE)

H20   -------. "Matheson in the Movies." <u>TZM</u> (September
       1981), pp. 51-54.
           Details of Matheson's career as a screenwriter.
       (SE)

H21   Mayer, Peter C. "Film, Ontology, and the Structure
       of a Novel." <u>Literature/Film Quarterly</u>, 8 (1980),
       204-08.
           A comparison of the film and the novel versions

of Slaughterhouse Five based on various aesthetic
theories of the nature of film (especially the use
of the photographic image). (PA)

H22   Newsome, Ted. "The Ray Harryhausen Story: Part One,
The Early Years, 1920-1958." Cinefantastique, 11
(December 1981), 24-45.
An unusually thorough essay which probes the
background and interests from Harryhausen's first
work and early career, with Harryhausen's comments
on each project and interviews with friends and
coworkers. (JS)

H23   Pattison, Patrick (See H28)

H24   Pitts, Michael R. Horror Film Stars. Jefferson,
NC: McFarland, 1981.
The first reference book to focus on both the
universally recognized great performers of the
horror film genre and the many important lesser
featured players who gave these films their special
"feel." Section 1 covers fifteen top stars: biography, career review, and complete filmography.
Section 2 covers twenty-eight additional film players in a like manner. Contains a comprehensive
bibliography of secondary works and a list of horror
film periodicals. Also issued in paperback. (MBT)

H25   Pohl, Frederik, and Frederik Pohl IV. Science
Fiction: Studies in Film. New York: Ace, 1981 pbk.
An informal account of the development of science
fiction film, arranged chronologically from Melies'
A Trip to the Moon (1902) through the 1979 films.
Filled with quotes from people interviewed by the
authors and from printed sources. Detailed film
credits appear in blocks adjacent to the commentary.
A lively and informed study. (MBT)

H26   Pohl, Frederik IV (See H25)

H27   Prawer, S. S. "Book into Film: Dr. Jekyll and Mr.
Hyde." Times Literary Supplement, 21 December 1979,
pp. 161-64.
A careful, analytic, informed comparison of
various adaptations of Jekyll and Hyde to the
screen, focussing on Rouben Mamoulian's 1932 version
starring Fredric March. (PA)

H28   Reed, Donald A., and Patrick Pattison. Collector's
Edition: Science Fiction Film Awards. La Habre, CA:
ESE California, 1981.
A pictorial description of the films, actors, and
actresses who have won recognition from the Academy
of Science Fiction, Fantasy, and Horror Films during
the period 1972-79. Also issued in paperback.
(MBT)

H29   Roth, Lane. "The Rejection of Rationalism in Recent
       Science Fiction Films." Philosophy in Context, 11
       (1981), 42-55.
            Argues that the image of the spaceship in recent
       science fiction films represents not an affirmation
       of mechanical order or faith in progress but a
       "denial of rationalism . . . an obstacle to be
       eliminated or a limitation to be transcended."
       (TPD)

H30   Sammon, Paul M. "David Cronenberg." Cinefantas-
       tique, 10 (Spring 1981), 20-35.
            Interview-essay covering all of Cronenberg's
       early work. (JS)

H31   Scigaj, Leonard M. "Bettelheim, Castaneda and Zen:
       The Powers Behind the Force in Star Wars." Extrap-
       olation, 22 (1981), 213-30.
            In Star Wars and The Empire Strikes Back, much of
       the attraction is the child's discovery/acceptance
       of power and responsibility. The process fits
       Bettelheim's description of fairy tales' role in the
       life of a child. The content fits Castaneda's
       account of the initiation process of "sorcerer,"
       with some influence of Zen as well. (JS)

H32   Seligson, Tom. "George Romero: Revealing the Mon-
       sters within Us." TZM (August 1981), pp. 12-17.
            An interview with the director of Night of the
       Living Dead (1969). (SE)

H33   Smith, Jeff. "Careening Through Kubrick's Space."
       Chicago Review, 33 (Summer 1981), 62-74.
            The close thematic connection between two Kubrick
       films (The Shining, 2001) is analyzed. The philo-
       sophical parallels in each show Kubrick occupied
       with "God, sin, and redemption in a narrative less
       linear that visually suggestive." (PA)

H34   Stanley, John. The Creature Features Movie Guide.
       Pacifica, CA: Creatures at Large, 1981 pbk.
            An alphabetized listing of 2,753 science fiction,
       fantasy, and horror films, with brief commentary on
       each. A handy guide, but not a comprehensive refer-
       ence tool. (MBT)

H35   Strickland, A. W., and Forrest J. Ackerman. A
       Reference Guide to American Science Fiction Films.
       Vol. 1. Bloomington, IN: T. I. S. Publications,
       1981.
            The first of a projected four-volume reference
       work which will systematically classify and annotate
       all science fiction films produced in the United
       States since 1897. Arranged by decade, the first
       volume covers the periods 1897-1909, 1910-1919, and
       1920-1929. The major strengths of this work are its
       attempt at subclassification of the films and the
       use of reference codes which key each film to

eighty-nine sources which aid in locating further
information on each film. (MBT)

H36   Sutton, David. "The Cinema of Roman Polanski."
       Dark Horizons, No. 22 (1981), pp. 24-30.
       An examination of Polanski's films and the theme
       of mental disintegration which runs throughout his
       work. (JF)

H37   Taylor, Martin. "SF on Television." Vector, No.
       102 (1981), pp. 8-17.
       Television is an important medium through which
       the public can be educated in good science fiction;
       but cultural influences create negative attitudes
       which prevent this from happening. The historical
       reasons for these attitudes, the nature of televi-
       sion, and the problems it presents for showing
       science fiction, are examined. (JF)

H38   Titterington, P. L. "Kubrick and The Shining."
       Sight and Sound, 150 (1981), 117-21.
       This analysis of Kubrick's work demonstrates the
       theme of isolation that runs through many of his
       films. (PA)

H39   Whetmore, Edward. "A Female Captain's Enterprise:
       The Implications of Star Trek's 'Turnabout Intrud-
       er.'" In Future Females. Ed. Marleen S. Barr.
       Bowling Green, OH: Bowling Green State Univ. Popular
       Press, 1981, pp. 157-61.
       Suggests we not label as sexist those literary
       criteria media spectacles created by a different
       aesthetic. (TPD)

H40   Wood, Denis. "The Empire's New Clothes." Film
       Quarterly, 34 (Spring 1981), 10-16.
       An analysis of two George Lucas films, Star Wars
       and The Empire Strikes Back, which criticizes the
       filmmaker for using the same formula over again.
       The differences between the two films, says Wood,
       are negligible. (PA)

I. Writing and Publishing

I01   Asimov, Isaac. "Editorial: Magazine Covers." <u>IASFM</u> (September 1981), pp. 5-10.
       The how and why of the design of science fiction magazine covers and the names of the magazines, starting with <u>Amazing</u> in 1926, with emphasis on the evolution of the cover of Asimov's own magazine. (TWH)

I02   Bova, Ben. <u>Notes to a Science Fiction Writer</u>. 2nd ed. Boston: Houghton Mifflin, 1981 pbk.
       Originally published by Charles Scribner's in 1975, this book offers basic advice to new writers. Bova examines four key story elements: character, background, conflict, and plot. Includes the text of four of Bova's own stories which serve as models for his discussion. This edition adds a chapter on the science fiction market and a revised bibliography. (MBT)

I03   Budrys, Algis. "Obstacles and Ironies in Science Fiction Criticism." <u>The Patchin Review</u>, No. 2 (1981), pp. 5-15.
       Discusses the limitations of effectiveness of science fiction book reviewing and criticism, using Damon Knight as the first to make science fiction critically self-conscious. (JS)

I04   Disch, Thomas M. "Science Fiction vs. Literature: The Prosecution's Case." <u>The Patchin Review</u>, No. 2 (1981), pp. 18-23.
       Uses reviews of his own books to show the cruel dilemma facing science fiction writers: give up concern with characterization and possibly negative conclusions, or risk hostility and neglect. (JS)

I05   Elgin, Suzette Hadin. "Informal Intro to Doing SF Poetry Workshops." <u>Starline</u>, No. 1 (1980), pp. 10-14.
       Provides guidance for obtaining a room, creating a program, scheduling, subject matter, funding, and all other matters related to organizing a science fiction poetry workshop, either in conjunction with a convention or independently. (TWH)

I06   Ellison, Harlan. "A Punk Is Not a Pistolero." <u>The Patchin Review</u>, No. 1 (1981), pp. 6-13.

Chiefly a challenge to John Shirley (whom Ellison accuses of criticizing him) to a writing match. Also comments on the competition between writers and on mistaken levels of prestige in science fiction—using Fritz Leiber as an example of one much under-valued. (JS)

I07   Gallun, Raymond Z. "The Profession of Science Fiction, 24: The Making of a Pulp Writer." Foundation, No. 22 (1981), pp. 35-48.
      A first-person reflection (as recorded by Jeffrey M. Elliot) covering biographical details and work habits of this veteran writer who is beginning to write and publish again. (DMH)

I08   Kadrey, Richard. ". . . but does T. S. Eliot belong in little plastic eggs?" SFWA Bulletin, No. 76 (1981), pp. 42-48.
      Sobering description of big business marketing practices for books. (JS)

I09   Koontz, Dean R. How To Write Best-Selling Fiction. Cincinnati: Writer's Digest, 1981.
      Contains a chapter on writing science fiction and mysteries. (MBT)

I10   Le Guin, Ursula K. "On Writing Science Fiction." The Writer, 94 (February 1981), 11-14.
      A noted writer of the genre gives her views emphasizing that science fiction is not the mindless macho space opera with which it is so often associated. In science fiction there is a rational reason for what happens; it must not contradict what is known to be known. (PA)

I11   Lewis, David. "SF in Japan." Locus, No. 250 (1981), p. 14.
      A survey of publishing and fandom in Japan, describing the collapse of a recent boom. (JS)

I12   Malzberg, Barry N. "Con Sordino." The Patchin Review, No. 1 (1981), pp. 4-5, 26.
      Deplores current blandness of science fiction. Malzberg suspects the origin is replacement of editors by people who simply want to move upward in a publishing career and who have little interest in what they are publishing and have no motivation to experiment. (JS)

I13   Martin, George R. R. "Sins of the Reviewers." Starship, No. 41 (1981), pp. 25-29.
      Making the distinction between the work of critics and the work of reviewers, Martin suggests that even with reviews the use of plot summaries is one of the "high crimes against literature." (DMH)

I14   Schweitzer, Darrell. "On Science Fiction Work-shops." IASFM (March 1981), pp. 101-08.

Describes the main science fiction workshops and
their techniques of teaching, with recommendations
for further reading. (TWH)

I15 Scithers, George H., et al. On Writing Science
     Fiction (The Editors Strike Back!). Philadelphia:
     Owlswick Press, 1981.
     The collective experience of the editors of Isaac
     Asimov's Science Fiction Magazine, distilled into a
     writer's guide. Separate chapters cover Idea, Plot,
     Character, Background, Science, Tragedy, and Comedy.
     Twelve stories, each a first sale by its author,
     have been selected to illustrate the main points of
     the book. (MBT)

I16 Silverberg, Robert. "Opinion." Amazing (July
     1981), pp. 6-7.
     A discussion and analysis of the effects on
     writers of the extensive feedback and interactions
     available with readers in the science fiction field
     which no other genre can offer. (TWH)

I17 Sky, Kathleen. "Finding Science Fiction Ideas."
     The Writer, 94 (May 1981), 17-18.
     Writers can find science fiction ideas by learn-
     ing about the past, "a repository of future cultures
     and source of nifty plots." Acquiring knowledge of
     the past means doing research, and Sky offers some
     helpful hints in this technique for budding authors.
     (PA)

I18 Teitelbaum, Sheldon. "SF in Israel." Locus, No.
     251 (1981), pp. 11-12.
     Describes the national personality as it affects
     publishing--readers in Israel, because of their
     pragmatic nature, prefer science fiction, not fan-
     tasy. Also comments on magazine publishing and on
     the birth of fandom. (JS)

I19 Thomas, Pascal J. "SF in France." Locus, No. 243
     (1981), p. 9.
     Publishing practices as they affect translations
     and original French science fiction. (JS)

I20 Wagner, Karl Edward. "Celluloid S & S: Boon or
     Menace?" FN, No. 42 (1981), pp. 6-8.
     Discusses cyclic nature of sword-and-sorcery
     publishing, its popularity killed each time by a
     flood of hackwork. Fears effects of current, movie-
     fanned popularity. (JS)

I21 Watson, Ian. "Into the Arena: 1. Down the Mine."
     Arena, No. 12 (1981), pp. 24-27.
     Concerned with the plight of the science fiction
     wirter whose work is mislabeled/misread and who is
     under ecomomic pressure to do marketable work he
     doesn't believe in. (JS)

I22   Weinberg, Robert. "Collecting Fantasy." FN, No. 33
       (1981), pp. 14-17.
          A discussion of Fantasy Press, focusing on the
       rarity/collectability of its books. Contains a
       chronological checklist of hardcovers published by
       Fantasy Press. (JS)

I23   -------. "Collecting Fantasy." FN, No. 36 (1981),
       pp. 14-16.
          A history of Weird Tales' sister magazine,
       Oriental Stories/Magic Carpet, which published a few
       straight fantasies but which featured exotic adven-
       ture tales by many fantasy writers--Howard, Quinn,
       Price, and others. (JS)

I24   -------. "Collecting Fantasy." FN, No. 40 (1981),
       pp. 15-17.
          A discussion of esoteric collectables, including
       art portfolios, publishers' and book clubs' mailers,
       unpublished manuscripts. (JS)

I25   -------. "Collecting Fantasy." FN, No. 41 (1981),
       pp. 7-9, 35.
          Discusses the Popular Publications reprint maga-
       zines--Famous Fantastic Mysteries, Fantastic Novels,
       and A. Merritt's Fantasy Magazine--including edit-
       orial scheduling and art buying. (JS)

I26   Williams, George L. "Italian Science Fiction for
       the 1980s." Extrapolation, 22 (1981), 191-95.
          Surveys contemporary Italian writing and publish-
       ing. (JS)

I27   Yong-lie, Ye. "SF in China, Part 1: American S. F.
       in China." Locus, No. 250 (1981), pp. 1, 15, 18.
          Publication of American science fiction in China,
       with a list of recent translations. (JS)

J. Teaching Resources

J01   Crossley, Robert. "Teaching the Course in Fantasy: An Elvish Counsel." Extrapolation, 22 (1981), 242-51.
      After wide experience teaching fantasy in a variety of settings, Crossley offers general advice on what to expect from students, what texts to use, and how the class may be taught and graded. (JS)

J02   Dubeck, Leroy W. "Science and Science Fiction Films." Journal of College Science Teaching, 11 (November 1981), 111-13.
      Describes a class taught as background for physics education; gives class format, sample class module, and syllabus listing films under different physical concepts. (TPD)

J03   Fantasy Literature [filmstrip-cassette]. Peoria, IL: Thomas S. Klise, 1981.
      Explains the nature and appeal of fantasy literature with illustrations from the works of its major writers. Includes a teacher's guide. (AT)

J04   Homer, David (See J08)

J05   Horror Fiction [filmstrip-cassette]. Peoria, IL: Thomas S. Klise, 1981.
      Explains the appeal of horror fiction by tracing it from its roots in the eighteenth-century Gothic novel to the twentieth-century interest in the occult. Includes a teacher's guide. (AT)

J06   Hull, Elizabeth Anne. "Take Me to Your Teacher." Destinies (Winter 1981), pp. 176-83.
      Provides help for prospective teachers of science fiction by listing and discussing national and regional forums for science fiction criticism and annual seminars specifically designed to teach teachers. (TPD)

J07   Krulik, Ted. "Science Fiction in the Classroom: Can Its Essence Be Preserved?" Extrapolation, 22 (1981), 155-63.
      How to teach an elective high school class, Junior and Senior level, keeping enjoyment by encouraging the free flow of ideas. (JS)

J08   Nunan, E. E., and David Homer. "Science, Science
      Fiction, and a Radical Science Education." SFS, 8
      (1981), 311-30.
           Contending that there exists a contradiction
      between the nature of modern science and how it is
      taught in school, the authors suggest a new educa-
      tional tool for "New Wave" science fiction in show-
      ing the social roots of how actual science works.
      (DMH)

J09   Roth, Lane. "Teaching Science Fiction Film Genre:
      Theory, Form, and Theme." Journal of English
      Teaching Techniques, 11 (1981), 42-56.
           A paradigm for teachers planning a course in
      science fiction film; discusses course structure and
      objectives, genre theory, the form of the science
      fiction film, and recurring themes. Provides a
      twenty-eight-segment syllabus, a list of films
      available for rent, and a reading list recommended
      for purchase by students. (TPD)

J10   Science Fiction Literature: The Quest for the
      Unknown [filmstrip-cassette]. Peoria, IL: Thomas S.
      Klise, 1981.
           Definition and history of science fiction,
      tracing it from Lucian of Samosata to the British
      New Wave. Includes a teacher's guide. (AT)

J11   Tymn, Marshall B. "Science Fiction and Fantasy in
      the School Curriculum: Part I: A Checklist of
      Articles, 1967-1975." English Language Arts
      Bulletin, 21 (Fall/Winter 1981), 24-27.
           A bibliography of articles directed toward the
      implementation of science fiction and fantasy in the
      public schools and universities. Items were selec-
      ted on the basis of their usefulness to the teacher,
      providing either background information or practical
      teaching suggestions. Each entry is annotated.
      (MBT)

J12   Wehmeyer, Lillian Biermann. Images in a Crystal
      Ball: World Futures in Novels for Young People.
      Littleton, CO: Libraries Unlimited, 1981.
           A resource book designed to assist teachers and
      librarians in using futuristic fiction as part of
      the study of science, social science, and litera-
      ture. Contents include a discussion of the role of
      futuristic literature in the classroom and library;
      a list of additional resource books; a survey of the
      range of ideas and inventions contained within
      certain works; an annotated bibliography of 150
      novels, written for grades eight and below; and an
      index of themes and motifs. (MBT)

J13   Wilton, Shirley M. "Juvenile Science Fiction
      Involves Reluctant Readers." Journal of Reading, 24
      (1981), 608-11.

Argues that the literary faults of science
fiction such as weak characterization, formula
situations, and emphasis on action, make the genre
accessible to reluctant readers accustomed to TV and
film. Lists science fiction for grades 3-5 and 6-9.
(TPD)

Author Index

Title Index